Festive
Christmas
Crafts

Carol Taylor

A Main Street Book

10 9 8 7 6 5 4 3 2 1

Published by Sterling Publishing Company, Inc.
387 Park Avenue South, New York, N.Y. 10016
Material for this collection has been taken from the following:
Treasures for the Christmas Tree © 1994 Altamont Press
Christmas Naturals © 1994 Altamont Press
Distributed in Canada by Sterling Publishing
% Canadian Manda Group, One Atlantic Avenue, Suite 105
Toronto, Ontario, Canada M6K 3E7
Distributed in Great Britain and Europe by Cassell PLC
Wellington House, 125 Strand, London WC2R 0BB, England
Distributed in Australia by Capricorn Link (Australia) Pty Ltd.
P.O. Box 6651, Baulkham Hills, Business Centre, NSW 2153, Australia

Printed in China
Sterling ISBN 0-8069-4789-6

Contents

Christmas Naturals

Ornaments, Wreaths & Decorations

INTRODUCTION

Of all the small ceremonies that make up a Christmas season, my favorite is the first one: unpacking the decorations.

Each December the members of my household go about their business, ignoring the green tinsel sprouting from the street lights and the carols yodeling through the stores. We wait for some inner clock to tell us when the season has arrived. Finally, someone says, "Wanna unpack the decorations?"

Yes! We grab a ladder and head for the hall closet, where whoever is feeling brave teeters on the highest rung and hands down the familiar boxes. One by one we unwrap the bells and wreaths and ornaments, remembering who gave us this, where we bought that, taking affectionate inventory of our friends, our family, and the Christmases we have spent together.

Then it's Christmas.

Making Your Own

In almost every household, the homemade decorations are the most fun to unpack. If we made them ourselves, they remind us of the evenings we spent up to our elbows in artemisia and glue. If they were gifts, they remind us of the giver—and of that little catch of breath ("You made this for me?") when someone makes us a present of their time and their creativity.

Making Christmas decorations isn't difficult. You don't need advanced degrees or special powers—just a few tools and materials, a couple of evenings, and a conviction that in the vast territory between "perfect" and "ugly," there's lots of room to maneuver.

Using Natural Materials

In this book, "natural materials" are plants or parts of plants: flowers and herbs both fresh and dried; evergreens and cones; spices and fruit; pods, seeds, grasses, and weeds. Some are cultivated. Others grow by the road, in the fields, or in the woods.

Working with natural materials changes the way you see. What used to look like scraggly brown weeds by the roadside, sad mementos of summer, now look like tall, graceful grasses with subtle colors and intricate shapes—perfect for a dried arrangement. You no longer wish someone would mow them down. You pick them instead.

Naturals can go rustic or elegant, and they can mix with glitzy accents without being outclassed. Wood mushrooms can hold their own with velvet ribbon. Deer moss is at least as well designed as gold mesh. You have only to glimpse a cluster of dry goldenrod backlit by the slanting winter sunlight to believe that natural materials are anything but shabby.

Where to Find Natural Materials

Craft stores. Most carry a fine selection of dried materials, some dyed, some left their natural color.

Florists. They stock up for Christmas with fresh and dried materials, some of which they'll sell you un-arranged.

Grocery stores. Many moderate-size supermarkets carry fresh flowers at reasonable prices. All have fresh fruit—apples, tangerines, pineapples, and grapes that are just as decorative as they are tasty. Keep an eye out for dried mushrooms, peppers, decorative gourds, and other interesting produce.

Backyard gardens. With the growing popularity of homemade wreaths and arrangements, all major seed companies carry such standards as artemisia, celosia, lavender, globe amaranth, and gypsophila (baby's breath). The seeds will do you no good this year but can make next year's decorations lavish.

Import marts. These are good sources of eucalyptus and dried grasses.

The world at large. In this book you'll find sumac heads cut behind a commercial car wash, moss gathered in a backyard, rabbit tobacco picked along an interstate highway, pine cones rescued from a restaurant parking lot, and rose hips gathered from a pasture hedgerow. Weeds are everywhere.

Harvesting Natural Materials

Once you begin to notice (and covet) natural materials, you may discover some new truths about yourself—not all of them pretty. I recently found myself eyeing some spectacular red berries by my bank's front door and wondering whether the bank manager would really mind if I "pruned" the bushes. Just as I was taking careful note of closing hours, I remembered the basic rules of courtesy in the field.

■ Before you pick on private property, ask. For all you know, the owner of that car wash cherishes those sumac heads and will be seriously displeased to discover you making off with them. Most of the time, people will be baffled that you even want their weeds and will enjoy being generous, but it's wise to check first.

■ Don't pick so much of anything that it can't come back next year. Rather than gathering all your ground pine from one patch, spread your picking out, taking a sprig here and there over a wide area.

■ Don't gather in public parks or campgrounds.

■ It almost (but not quite) goes without saying that if a plant is endangered, it should not be gathered at all. When posted signs plead with you to leave the sea oats on this particular beach, no ornament is worth it. The world is full (so far) of beautiful plants. After a momentary regret, you won't really miss this one.

How to Use This Book

Many of the projects in this book are the work of professional designers. Others are by enthusiastic amateurs. If a project suits you exactly, there's no reason not to duplicate it. Better yet, use the projects and the accompanying instructions for ideas and inspiration, then make something uniquely your own. And don't be deterred if some of the materials on any one project aren't readily at hand. If the globe amaranth crop was bad this year, substitute something else. If Fraser fir doesn't grow in your region, another greenery does—equally attractive, equally accessible.

Permission

One final caution: If you've always assumed that making Christmas decorations was something other people did—people with some mysterious talent you didn't possess— you may act a tad silly this year.

Let's say that your first project is a garland of boxwood and baby's breath, that it encircles the picture window in your living room, and that it's the single most gorgeous thing you've ever seen. You can't believe you made it. Fourteen times a day, you pass through the room, stop dead, and stare, with complete, unabashed admiration.

Eventually, you try to get a grip on yourself. Listen, you say, I've raised five children, I won the Nobel Prize in subatomic physics, I've lost four pounds. Why should I be so fatuously proud of one Christmas garland?

I don't know either. But it's okay. And if you'll show me yours, I'll show you mine.

CONTRIBUTING DESIGNERS

Julianne Bronder is a designer for Vans Floral Products in Alsip, Illinois. She studied at the American Floral Art School in Chicago and has taught floral design. (Pages 34, 46, 48, 49, 97, 108, 109, 112, and 113.)

Janet Frye owns The Enchanted Florist in Arden, North Carolina. Trained at Adam Eden Florist in Palm Springs, California, Janet has been a floral designer for 14 years and has taught design for seven. (Pages 17, 30, 31, 36, 37, 54, 55, 58, 64, 114, and 115.)

Fred Tyson Gaylor is a product designer at Hanford's, Inc., a wholesale holiday accessory company in Charlotte, North Carolina. He taught art in the public school for 10 years. (Pages 38, 100, 106, and 110.)

Cynthia Gilooley owns The Golden Cricket, a floral design studio in Asheville, North Carolina, where she enjoys whipping up slightly unconventional creations. (Pages 39 bottom, 43, 47, 56, and 60.)

Jeannette Hafner grows the flowers and greenery for her designs in her gardens in Orange, Connecticut. She teaches drying and arranging techniques as well as design classes. (Pages 69, 70, 71, 72, 73 top, 98, 99, 120, and 121.)

Carol Heller is a banker who resides in Durham, Connecticut, and enjoys designing with natural materials. (Pages 122, 123, 124, 125, and 127.)

Wana Henry, a craftsperson from Church Hill, Tennessee, works primarily with cones and seeds, and markets her work at craft fairs. (Pages 35 bottom, 79, 90, 91, and 93 bottom.)

Judy Horn specializes in corn husk crafts. With husband Dave, she owns The Corn Husk Shoppe in Weaverville, North Carolina, where she sells her corn husk flowers and dolls, along with wreaths and arrangements. (Pages 40, 41, 102, 103, and 107.)

Alyce Nadeau grows 200 different herbs for her business, Goldenrod Mountain Herbs, in Deep Gap, North Carolina. She designs a wide range of herbal items and has been known to arrange an herbal wedding, complete with food, beverage, and bouquets. (Pages 32, 68, 73 bottom, 74, 75, 80, 86, 87, 88, 89, and 126.)

Alan Salmon and **Betty Sparrow** own and operate Wildwood Herbal Flower Farm at Reems Creek, in Weaverville, North Carolina. They sell fresh and dried herbs and flowers, along with wreaths, bouquets, and flower baskets.

For the projects on pages 81 and 84, they enlisted the help of Alan's sister, Jeanne Whitaker. (The front cover and pages 35 top, 81, and 84.)

Sandy Mush Herb Nursery, Leicester, North Carolina, is the full-time passion of the Jayne family. They grow an extensive variety of culinary, decorative, and fragrant herbs, which they sell, along with their wreaths, through their mail-order catalogs. (Pages 39 top, 61, 62, 63, 85, 92 inset, 96, 111, 117, and 119.)

Diane Weaver worked as an art director/designer in Detroit and New York. With husband Dick, she operates Gourmet Gardens, an herb nursery in Weaverville, North Carolina. She uses some of the 180 herbs they grow to design and make wreaths, arrangements, culinary herb mixtures, and herb butters. (Pages 26, 28, 42, 44, 50, 52, 65, 66, 67, 76, 77, 78, 94, 104, 116, and 118.)

And thanks to . . .
Pat Barnes (pages 59, 92, and 93 top), Darlene Conti (82 and 83), Rasland Farms (33), Sarah Searcy (8 and 60), and Elly Shriver (128).

8

TOOLS & MATERIALS

GLUE GUNS

A glue gun may not be the most fun you can have for under $10, but it's close. Fast, easy to use, and incredibly flexible, it will affix almost anything to almost anything else.

For this book, designers used glue guns to attach flowers, herbs, cones, nuts, seeds, pods, bows, ribbons, lace, twigs, vines, lichens, and birds (fake, of course) to bases of foam, moss, vine, straw, and plastic.

To use a glue gun, simply insert a glue stick, plug in the gun, and wait for it to heat. Then aim and squeeze the trigger. Hold the glued items together for half a minute or so, until the bond is firm.

A few tips:

■ Cover the work area with newspaper. Almost all glue guns drip.
■ A glue gun that can stand up when you set it down is extremely convenient. When shopping for a gun, check to see whether it has a stand in front (some are detachable and included in the box) and whether the handle is designed to sit flat, increasing its stability and reducing the number of times you'll knock it over. If the gun has no stand, rest it on a ceramic plate or some other fireproof container between shots.

■ As you work, the gun will produce ethereal strands of glue that resemble spiderwebs. Just remember to pull them off the project when you're done.
■ If you're working with a plastic foam base, test a small area first. Almost all guns will melt foam, but some cause more damage than others. If a deep, moist crater appears on the base, cover it with moss, using floral greening pins. Then glue your materials to the moss.
■ Don't hesitate to use as much glue as you need. Many times a small dab will suffice, but some of the refined-looking projects in later chapters conceal globs of glue the size of calamata olives.
■ Anything that will melt foam can burn fingers; exercise some care. If you find that you burn yourself frequently, investigate the "warm melt" guns on the market. They use glue sticks that melt at a lower temperature and thus don't get as hot.
■ Unplug the gun as soon as you're finished, and never leave an unsupervised child around a gun.

FLORAL FOAM

Foam allows you to convert a pile of flowers into an arrangement and a bag of fruit into a wreath—in other words, the parts into a whole. Since foam isn't nearly as pretty as it is useful, it's at its best covered with greenery or flowers, providing an invisible means of support.

Foam comes in two forms: dry and wet. Each has advantages.

Dry. This is the rigid plastic foam (Styrofoam, for example) readily available in craft shops, discount houses, and department stores. It comes in a variety of shapes—sheets, cones, balls, squares, and rectangles—and is easily cut and shaped even further with a serrated knife.

It also comes in white or green. Given a choice, use whichever color blends best with the materials you're attaching (for example, a green foam base for an herbal wreath). That way, if a section does manage to peek through, it is less glaring.

Some blocks of foam come with a self-adhesive strip on the bottom, convenient for securing to a container—for example, the bowl that will hold an arrangement. If there's no strip, there's no problem. Floral tape, clay, or wire, a glue gun, or brute force will all work well.

Evergreens and flowers with tough stems can be inserted directly into the foam; just cut the stem at an angle to provide a pointed end. Weak-stemmed flowers must be attached to floral picks and then inserted (see page 12).

Wet. This fine-grained floral foam (touch it, and a fine dust comes off on your fingers) is invaluable for fresh arrangements. When soaked in water, it will absorb and hold moisture for weeks. Thus, fresh materials inserted into it can absorb moisture as they need it. Wet foam allows you to decorate a tabletop Christmas tree, for example, with fresh carnations (page 115) that will last through the season.

Wet-type foam comes in "bricks" like the one at the bottom left corner of the page.

Occasionally, designers use dry foam without wetting it, when they're working with especially delicate dried flowers, when they want an especially small piece of foam, or when there's nothing else around the house.

PICKS

A floral pick looks like an over-grown toothpick with a piece of thin, flexible wire attached to one end. Picks come in various sizes, most typically three inches or six inches long (7.5 or 15 cm.). They're available in unfinished wood or painted green, the latter being less visible in a thicket of foliage, and in craft shops and discount marts. A pick acts as an artificial stem. Its sharp end penetrates a variety of bases—foam, straw, and (less successfully) vine—and holds upright and stable whatever flimsy plant or odd-shaped item is attached to it. In a vine base, a pick must be reinforced with hot glue. Otherwise, either

it won't go in far enough or it wobbles around in the spaces between the coiled vines.

Materials can be attached to a pick by wire, glue, or simple jabbing. For wiring, hold the pick and a plant's stem together, making sure that whatever you want to be visible—the flower, the best greenery—is above the pick's wire. Tightly wrap the wire around both the stem and the pick, starting with several horizontal turns at the top and then spiraling down the length of the stem. You might want to snip off the stem if it extends beyond the pick, for easier insertion into the base.

For a more durable result, wrap the wired pick and stem with floral tape—just stretch and wrap. With this final step, the stem is less likely to be dislodged.

Follow a similar procedure for a small bunch of flowers or greenery. Arrange them into the bouquet you want, wrap the wire around the pick and all the stems, and finish off with floral tape.

If an object (a sturdy mushroom, for example) has nothing long, thin, and vertical to wire the pick to, you can hot-glue it to the top of the pick and go from there. In a pinch, you can even jam the top of the pick into an expendable item—for example, an apple or a tangerine—and call it art.

PINS

Floral pins—also known as "fern pins" or "greening pins"—are quick and easy to use. They will attach bunches of herbs or flowers to a straw base and moss of all sorts to a foam one, a task at which they excel.

A moss-covered base can be an integral part of the design—see the luxuriant wreath on page 30—or merely an insurance policy. Many designers cover a foam base with moss before adding any other materials, so that if the base accidentally peeks through, the viewer will see natural moss rather than naked foam. (The block of foam below is invisible under curly Spanish moss, which is attached with an equally invisible pin.) Moreover, it's often easier to hot-glue materials to moss than to meltable foam.

WIRE

A cone, a bow, even a bunch of grapes can be attached to a base with a piece of wire. Although common hardware-variety wire will work, floral wire—inexpensive, flexible, and green—is well worth a trip to your neighborhood craft shop or discount store. It comes in several thicknesses, or gauges, all of which are useful on various occasions. Attaching a small cone calls for the thinnest, most flexible wire you can find; forming the "spine" of a garland demands a heavy-duty gauge.

Wiring is especially useful on wreaths, since the base is a convenient diameter for wrapping wire around. A vine base is perfect; each coil of vine provides a point of purchase.

To wire an object, first look it over for an inconspicuous place to attach the wire. If there is none, plan to hide the wire later with other materials —a sprig of greenery, perhaps.

Fold a length of wire loosely in half and slip it around the object, with the ends of wire on the back side. Twist the strands of wire together, right next to the item, so that the object is held securely. Now hold it tightly against the base, with the two wires straddling the base. Again twist the strands until the object is held firmly in place. Reinforce with hot glue if necessary.

An especially delicate item— a small cone, for instance—may fare better if you carefully loop the end of the wire around it, leaving yourself a single long stem to wrap around (or insert into) the base.

To wire a piece of fruit—a lemon or tangerine, for example— pierce it with a heavy-gauge wire end-to-end, and wrap the ends of the wire around the base.

BASIC INSTRUCTIONS

MAKING WREATHS

Some people are born with nimble fingers, muscular egos, and a natural affinity for crafts. Then there's the rest of us, who remain dubious about the whole business well into adulthood. For us, a wreath is often our first craft project.

It finally dawns on us that anybody—anybody—can wind a red ribbon around a straw base, insert a few sprigs of greenery and some silver bells, and hang on the front door a decoration that we made, by George, ourselves.

After that first confidence-building wreath, we branch out into other bases, other means of attachment, other materials, other locations, and, frequently, other crafts.

Bases. Even small crafts stores stock a variety of wreath bases: straw, moss, vine, foam, wire, paper, even rattan. In December, foam bases covered with ground cinnamon appear in some craft shops. Sizes range from tiny to huge.

Attachment. Gluing, picking, wiring, pinning—all are legitimate means of getting natural materials to stay where you want them.

Materials. Evergreens, flowers fresh or dried, berries, cones, fruit, nuts, seedheads, pods—if it's pretty enough for you to lean down and pick up, it's wreath material. (Assuming, of course, reasonable size and weight. Fenceposts are probably out.)

Locations. Wreaths have traditionally graced front doors and mantlepieces, but they also look good elsewhere: interior doors, walls, windows, cabinets, and every room of the house, even the bath.

An outside wreath invites your guests inside, whether it's hanging on an exterior wall, a gatepost, a lamppost, or even a tree close to the house.

Tips
All of these suggestions for applying materials are violated regularly and deliberately, with splendid results. But they're still good general rules.

■ Start with your background material—something you have lots of, which covers well, and which you like (it will be prominent in the wreath). Possibilities include moss (see page 30), silver king artemisia (page 35), boxwood (page 26), bay leaves (page 44), and sorghum heads (page 37).

■ Usually, materials should be inserted into the base at the same angle. In the wreath on page 34, for example, carefully angled eucalyptus sprigs produce a pinwheel effect.

■ Framing the outside of the wreath can be effective. For example, on page 47 magnolia leaves encircle the wreath, providing a frame for the apples and grapes.

■ If the base is attractive, part of it—even most of it—can be left bare. Vine bases are interesting and complex, either natural (page 43) or misted with paint (page 39), and pine needle bases are attractively rough and rustic (page 40).

But bare sections need to be deliberate. Unintended bare patches will spoil a wreath. In applying background material, overlap the picked or wired bunches as you go around the wreath, thus covering the base thoroughly.

MAKING ARRANGEMENTS

Foam. Choose either dry foam, for dried arrangements, or wet foam, for fresh materials, and cut it to fit the container. Make sure the foam is taller than the sides of the bowl, so that you can insert materials into it horizontally. For extra security, tape the foam to the pot.

(Some stores carry a type of floral tape made especially for wet form.)

Container. As long as it's stable and will hold a piece of foam large enough to support all the materials you plan to use, the container can be just about anything: vase, flowerpot, pitcher, bowl. Reconnoiter your cupboard. You may find favorite pieces that can be brought out of the closet and used.

Sometimes a container-within-a-container is the solution. Baskets make handsome holders for natural materials, but they're often too large and oddly shaped to fill with foam, always too leaky and easily water-stained to hold fresh flowers. Place a piece of foam in a bowl, the bowl in the basket, and crumpled newspaper around the sides, to hold the bowl in place.

The designer of the partridge in the pear tree on page 110 wanted to hold a tree branch upright in plaster of Paris, but he certainly didn't want to harden plaster in a good brass urn. So he poured the plaster into a cheap plastic pot, placed that inside the urn, and saved his brass.

Shape. An arrangement needs an overall shape: triangular, for example, or oval, or round. Whether you make yours vertical or horizonal may depend on where you intend to display it. For example, the horizontal arrangement on page 52 echoes the lines of the table it sits on.

The overall shape may be defined completely by the materials themselves, or the eye may be allowed to fill in the gaps. The triangle on page 59 is unmistakable; every inch of it is filled with plants. But the arrangement on page 58 is also triangular. Between the tip of the taller candle and the tips of the cedar branches on each side there's nothing much but air. Still, those three points form the perimeter of the arrangement, and the eye connects them—one reason this arrangement is so satisfying.

Color. When most of us look at grapes, red onions, and orchids, we see fruit, vegetables, and flowers. One designer looked at them and saw purple—which is how they all ended up in the arrangement on page 56.

As you look for natural materials, try defining them, not in the usual way, but as colors. You may find that you quite literally see things differently, and stumble upon materials you would otherwise never have thought to use.

Application. Generally, it's useful to establish the boundaries of the

arrangement first—to insert the flower or greenery that will provide the highest point, then the materials that will define the outside diameter. With the general shape to guide you, go back and fill in the arrangement.

It's also useful to apply heavy or bulky materials before light, delicate ones. For one thing, the materials are less likely to be damaged that way.

In the arrangement pictured, the designer first inserted the carnations (the highest one first) into the wet foam. With the perimeters drawn, she filled in with bulky galax leaves, then with poms, and, finally, with featherweight spengeri fern.

Focal point. Many arrangements have one component so eye-catching that it inevitably becomes the focal point of the arrangement—all eyes immediately focus on it. If you plan to use a showy bow, for example, or a large, spectacular flower, give some thought to exactly where it should be.

Angle. Consider the height at which the arrangement will be displayed—a high mantlepiece, a low coffee table, a waist-high sideboard—and work on it at that angle. Otherwise, no one may see its best side.

Candles. Metal or plastic candle holders are widely available, ready to insert into the base. Another option is to tape two floral picks to the candle. Not only is a picked candle more stable, but the base takes up less room in the arrangement.

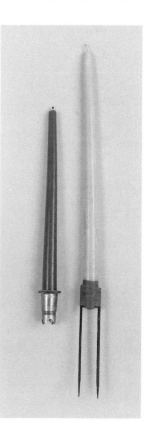

MAKING GARLANDS

Perhaps it's all those Victorian woodcuts of merrymakers in long gowns and frock coats, draping greenery down a banister. Whatever the reason, when we plan to deck the halls, we think inevitably of garlands.

Making a garland entails attaching decorative materials to a long "spine"—something thin, flexible, and tough.

Most children have strung cranberries for the tree, using ordinary needle and thread. That's a garland, and it can be combined with others and used other places (see page 104). Variations abound. Tough little globe amaranth blossoms can be strung the same way, for a brilliant result (page 84), as can anything else that's sturdy enough to be pierced without falling apart.

If you're dealing with materials that are not conveniently round, you'll need a different spine and a different means of attachment.

Heavy-gauge wire makes a good, durable spine, but the favorite of many designers is jute cord—the type used for macrame. Cut the cord a little longer than you want the garland to be. Some people tie it between two supports—two chair backs, for example—at a comfortable working height; others prefer a work table or the floor.

Wherever you choose to work, form a small bunch of greenery and/or flowers (half a dozen stems or so) and wire the stems together. Then wire the bunch to the spine, using fine, spool-type floral wire. Then wire on another bunch, overlapping the previous one. Continue down the length of the cord, until the garland is finished.

The artistry comes in the composition of the bunches. You can make bunches of individual materials and alternate them down the garland—one bunch of Fraser fir, then one of blue spruce, then gypsophila, then repeat—or each bunch can be composed of several different materials.

After the garland is complete, decorative accents—berries, Christmas balls, knickknacks— can be hot-glued in place. A bow can be wired at either end, at the center, or both.

MAKING SWAGS

Broadly defined, swags are bouquets designed to hang—on a wall, a door, a chimney, a cabinet. They can range from beautifully simple to strikingly complex.

Vertical bouquets. The simplest swag consists of greenery or flowers wired together by the stems, usually with a bow wired on to cover the attached stems. Since the design is predictable, all attention focuses on the materials, which need to be very attractive if this decoration is to work. The traditional swag on page 97, for example, displays very fresh, very colorful Christmas greenery to good advantage.

Horizontal bouquets. Not just bouquets hung by their "ankles," horizonal swags are somewhat more complicated to make (but not much). Usually, background material—for example, the ever-popular silver king artemisia on page 98—is divided into two bunches, which are placed end to end, with their foliage to the right and left, their stems in the center. With these stems overlapped and wired together, additional materials are wired or hot-glued on, radiating from the center and following the basic shape. A bow wired in the center hides the wired stems.

Backing. A third type of swag consists of materials attached to a solid backing that gives the decoration shape. The heavy door swag on page 106 has a backing of foam glued onto a board.

Found objects. Some of the most intriguing swags consist of an object decorated with natural materials. Anything interesting will serve: a cinnamon broom (page 107), a garlic braid (page 94), even an antique sickle (page 109). This is perhaps the most imagination-stretching swag to put together: spotting an everyday object that, with a little dressing up, is worth displaying.

MAKING TREES

Poet Joyce Kilmer wrote that "only God can make a tree," but then he'd never heard of Styrofoam. If you're trying for only a tabletop model, you have lots of options.

Vine. Vine trees are widely available in craft stores or Christmas shops, ready to be decorated to your taste. Or you can make your own. Gather a good quantity of thin, dried vines—honeysuckle, grapevine, wisteria, whatever grows where you are. (Note: If you're allergic to poison ivy or oak, you will react to the dry vines as you do to the green leaves. It's wise to know what you're getting into.) Another option is to buy a vine wreath and uncurl it.

However you get them, soak the vines for four or five hours, to soften them. Make a cone-shaped cardboard form, and wrap the pliable vines around it. Allow to dry overnight, and remove the tree from its form.

Foam. Plastic foam cones, widely available, supply ready-made tree shapes. They're stable enough to stand upright on their own, and materials can be inserted or picked directly into them, following the basic tree shape. The one shown has boxwood stems inserted into the top and a piece of ground pine picked into the bottom. A cone can also be glued to the end of an upright tree branch for a Douglas fir shape (see page 110, for example).

A brick of wet floral foam, stood on end, makes a good base for a tree that includes fresh materials. Tape the foam securely to a shallow container, making the tape bite into the foam, and insert materials so that they form a tree shape. Water the tree from the top, for a long-lasting decoration.

Foam balls are also useful for a topiary style of tree. Hot-glued to the top of a tree branch, they can make an interesting double tree (see page 112).

Faux tree. (Please. Not "artificial," but "faux." You may be faking it, but you're faking it with class.) A green plastic tree looks undeniably fake, but if it's covered with natural materials, no one will know. (Check out pages 120 and 121, and be honest; could you tell?) Faux trees are so inexpensive and convenient that even the most committed naturalists buy them and hot-glue natural materials onto them.

Plants. Live plants that are naturally tree-shaped—or can be pruned that way—make interesting table trees. A cactus, for example, or a rosemary plant (page 116) can turn into a Christmas tree overnight.

MAKING ORNAMENTS

An ornament can be a single interesting item—for example, a milkweed pod—attached to an ornament hanger with a dab of hot glue. It can be a small bunch of berries, dried flowers, or grasses tied with ribbon. It can be a foam or glass ball with natural materials glued onto it.

Walk around your yard, wander through the woods, and scan the roadsides as you drive, redefining what you see. Is that a Christmas ornament that no one else has recognized?

Then head for the crafts store, scanning not just the Christmas section but other areas as well. Small baskets offer endless possibilities, as do other miniature containers (flowerpots, toy watering cans, wheelbarrows, kitchen implements). The dried materials are worth considering: a lotus pod makes an interesting ornament (see page 89).

Tips
■ Think light. An ornament doesn't have to be very heavy at all to make a fir branch as droopy as the post-Christmas blues.
■ Keep in mind that the ornament will be displayed on a green tree. Unless the observer is very close indeed, or the texture is markedly different, greenery on an ornament won't show up.
■ Be sure to attach the hanger (whether ribbon or wire) so that the ornament will hang with the correct side out. Since tree branches usually project out from the center of the tree, most hangers should go from side to side, rather than from front to back.
■ An excellent hanger for foam balls is a "hairpin" made of heavy-gauge floral wire, stuck into the ball. A commercial wire hanger can attach to that.

DECORATING PACKAGES

A present that is hand-decorated with natural materials sends a special warmth. It makes a gift, not only of the contents, but of your time and creativity as well.

To create distinctive packages, you'll need only natural materials and a glue gun. After wrapping the package with paper in the normal fashion, position the materials in a pleasing arrangement, and hot-glue them to the paper or to each other. If desired, add a bow or mix in some artificial fruit, berries, or a small bird.

Tips

■ Consider the package as a whole: the paper, the natural materials, and (if you're using one) the ribbon. Make sure the colors of paper and the naturals complement each other.

■ When selecting natural materials, try for a variety of shapes and textures. On the package below, fuzzy strawflowers and rigid pine cones provide contrasting textures.

■ Arrange the natural materials in an identifiable shape—a crescent, circle, or rectangle, for example. It helps to do a few dry runs, laying out the materials in a variety of combinations on a scrap of paper before actually gluing them down.

■ Start with relatively flat background materials, then add the more three-dimensional items.

■ Packages can be wrapped in fabric, rather than paper, with natural materials hot-glued on in the same fashion—often with memorable results.

MAKING CORN HUSK FLOWERS

The cinnamon-broom swag on page 107 and the wreaths on pages 40 and 41 get part of their charm from corn husk flowers. The blooms may look complicated, but they're not difficult to make.

Corn husks can be purchased at craft stores or shucked from actual ears of corn. If you peel your own, be careful not to tear the husks as you remove them; the larger the husks, the easier they are to work with. Spread them in the sun to dry, keeping them in a thin layer and turning them often, so they'll dry quickly without mildew.

If you want colored flowers, fabric dyes work well on corn husks. Dissolve approximately half a package of dye in half a gallon of water, and heat to boiling. (Actual amounts can vary with the stiffness of the husks and the amount of natural yellow they have.) Dip the husks in the hot dye. If you want a deep hue, remove the dye from the heat and let the husks soak overnight.

Looped Flowers

1. Tear your stiffest husks lengthwise into strips. You'll need five strips about 1-3/4 inches (4.4 cm.) wide for the petals.

2. Use your less attractive husks to make the center. Roll the husks into a roll about 3/4 inch in diameter, and wire with firm wire about an inch (2.5 cm.) from the top. Trim the wire ends and excess corn husk, leaving about an inch of husk below the wire.

3. Fold the petal strips in half and position them around the center. Wire them to the center either one by one or all at once, whichever is easier.

4. Trim excess husks from the bottom, tapering the base instead of cutting straight across.

5. Cut a piece of heavy wire about 18 inches (45 cm.) long. Make a "fish hook" in one end and insert the other end into the center. Carefully pull the wire down through the flower until the hook anchors in the center. Tape the flower to the wire with masking tape, covering the flower's tapered base and about 1/2 inch (1.25 cm.) of the wire. Wrap the base and the entire stem with floral tape. (See the shaggy flower below.)

Shaggy Flowers

1. Gather pieces of husk in a bundle, with the natural points in the same direction. The fatter the bundle, the larger the flower. A good working diameter is two inches (5 cm.).

2. Wire the bundle tightly with heavy floral wire about 5-1/2 inches (13.75 cm.) from the top (the pointed ends), and trim off excess husk, tapering the cut.

3. Tear the husks into large strips.

Or shred the husks with a hat pin, for a wispy, curly effect. Shredded husks will curl naturally as they continue to dry.

4. Add a stem as described for the looped flowers. The stem can remain beautifully long and straight, for arrangements, or twist around a wreath base for anchoring.

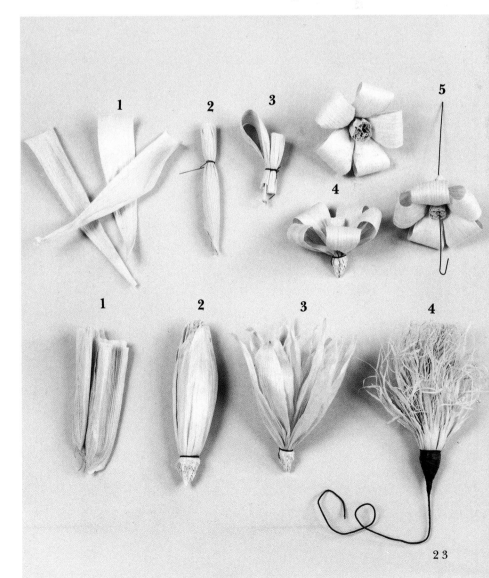

MAKING BOWS

To have tried to make a bow is to understand despair. The ribbon seems to take on a life (and a passive-aggressive personality) of its own, wriggling out of your fingers one moment, lying there limply the next. And it's small comfort that every smart-aleck you talk to says there's nothing to it.

There's nothing to it. Especially at Christmas, craft stores stock ready-made, red velvet bows in various sizes and will probably make you a bow of any ribbon in stock.

On the other hand, there are wonderful ribbons—watered silk, paper, raffia, taffeta, grosgrain, metallic, net, lace, velvet cord, satin tapestry—sold by places that do not make bows. If you do, you can turn a good project into a smashing one.

Picked Loops

An easy option is to wire loops of ribbon onto floral picks. Just fold a piece of ribbon loosely in half, pinch the ends together against a pick, and wrap the wire around the ribbon. The picked loops at the lower left of this page were made three different ways: with a tail, with two loops, and with a single loop.

To create a bow, pick the loops into the base of your project, one on top of the other. In the arrangement on page 54, the bow at the lower left consists of three picked loops.

Real Bows

1. Form a circle at the end of the ribbon. (The one in the photo is lying on its side.)

2. Pinch the circle together in the center, and hold it there. This is even easier than it sounds.

3. Adding to the back of the bow, form loops of ribbon, first on one side, then the other, continuing until the bow is as full as you want it. This is harder than it sounds.

4. Wire the bow together in the center, leaving long enough wire ends for attaching to the project.

5. Shape the bow, pulling the loops into position. Move a loop around by inserting your finger inside it and pulling; if you pinch the loop closed, it will flatten.

Tips

■ The key words are "pinch and twist."

As you complete each new loop by bringing the ribbon back to the center of the bow, pinch the ribbon in the middle and twist it, so that the upper side becomes the lower one. Otherwise, half of the loops will be wrong-side-out.

■ A bow wired onto a pick is often easier to insert in an arrangement or wreath.

■ Don't underestimate the amount of ribbon you'll need. A decent-sized bow can eat up four yards of ribbon without even trying.

■ Learning to make bows is largely a matter of fiddling with a ribbon until until you like the result, then repeating the process until you've got it down. It's not a bad way to spend a rainy afternoon.

This three-foot-long (90 cm.) wreath can decorate even the largest fireplace without looking skimpy. The base is heavy, galvanized clothesline wire shaped into an oval, with the ends overlapped about three inches (7.5 cm.) and taped together with duct tape. Bunches of boxwood—three or four branches about 12 inches (30 cm.) long wired together—were wired to the base, starting at the bottom and working up one side, overlapping the bunches to cover the stems of the previous bunch. The other side was then covered in a similar manner. Three-inch burgundy cockscomb heads were hot-glued close to the base of the boxwood bunches, using lots of glue. The rest of the materials were then hot-glued at random to the branches: white strawflowers, sprigs of baby's breath, red globe amaranth, and holly leaves that had been gilded with a paint pen. A bow made from three yards (2.8 m.) of wired burgundy ribbon was wired to the top of the wreath, and its streamers woven down the sides.

When the Christmas spirit strikes late, ready-made bases are invaluable time-savers. Embellished with natural materials, plain evergreen wreaths and garlands can become uniquely your own.

To make a wreath and garland like the ones shown, first prepare the flowers and fruit. Cut five three-inch (7.5 cm.) green foam balls in half, and hot-glue colorful flowers over the spherical sides. Six of those pictured are covered with globe amaranth; four, with celosia. Then wire the dried pomegranates: run a seven-inch (17.5 cm.) piece of wire through the center of each fruit, top to bottom. Make a fish hook on the bottom, and pull it back into the fruit, anchoring it firmly.

Wire a few sprigs of boxwood or other greenery around the wreath, for variety in the foliage. Wire the pomegranates to the wreath, and hot-glue on the flower-foam balls, spacing them evenly.

Make a bow with long streamers from four yards (3.7 m.) of wired net ribbon and wire it to the top, trailing the streamers around the wreath. Hot-glue sprigs of yarrow, clusters of pepperberries, and additional amaranth and celosia to the foliage.

Arrange the swag in position on the mantle, then attach the flowers. Pick small bunches of red-dyed bunnytails, globe amaranth, and celosia into the branches, and hot-glue sumac heads to the sides. Wire a bow to the center, and weave the ribbon ends in and out of the swag. Finally, hot-glue globe amaranth, peppers, yarrow, and zinnias over the entire swag.

LEFT: Be prepared: when you put velvety green moss on a wreath, people are going to fondle it. Fresh sheet moss covers this 14-inch (35 cm.) straw base, which the designer attached with floral pins. She then wired a small piece of rigid foam to the top, providing a point of purchase for flowers, and wrapped metallic-gold wired ribbon around the wreath, with the ends pinned in place. The same ribbon supplied a bow. (To curl the streamers, wrap the ribbon around a candle, a dowel, or your finger.) Flowers and berries are attached to the foam in a crescent shape: first the miniature myrtle and German statice, then rose hips, then dried asters and roses. Small accent pieces are hot-glued to the lower right.

BELOW: In late fall, rose hips still cling to the leafless branches of rose bushes, both tame and wild. They make colorful Christmas wreaths. For this one, the designer hot-glued branches of rose hips onto a vine base and then added small cedar tips, tucking them around and under the berries and attaching them with a glue gun. A scattering of cone "roses" finished the wreath.

If you can't lay your hands on any rose hips, bittersweet berries will also work. Just peel off the outer, gold-colored petal.

LEFT: All ready to hang on a headboard or bedroom wall, this graceful wreath has a grapevine base. After hot-gluing 10 sprigs of eucalyptus around the base at an angle, the designer made small bouquets of hydrangea by taping their stems together, and glued them around the base, carefully inserting the stems of the last bunch under the head of the first one. She then hot-glued a ribbon in loops around the outside, with each loop beginning and ending halfway between the eucalyptus sprigs. Sprigs of baby's breath hot-glued around the outside finished the wreath.

BELOW: Fragrant sweet Annie formed the base for this floral wreath. The greenery was wrapped around a wooden pegged frame, then removed from the frame and tied with floral wire. The dried flowers were affixed to the base with tacky glue: miniature roses, lavender, blue salvia, celosia, statice, strawflowers, and globe amaranth.

Long, striped protea pods steal the show in this mix of materials. The straw base is wrapped with strapping tape to provide extra support. Sprigs of eucalyptus, picked around the wreath at an angle, supply the background; picked okra and protea pods add interest. Protea foliage, German statice, and faux red berries, hot-glued around the wreath, add variety and color.

wreath shape makes a perfect base; just wire the cones, insert the wire ends into two adjacent holes, and twist. Hot-glue nuts around the wreath at attractive intervals.

Clip long wires on the back and attach a wire hanger. It's helpful to cover the back: cut out a "dough-nut" of felt and glue it on. The wreath can either hang on a wall or sit on a table, with a fat candle in the center.

LEFT: The scents of this herbal wreath linger on the air without overpowering all who come near. Small bunches of dried sage, mint, southernwood, and silver king artemisia were wired together, then pinned around a straw base with floral pins, with the bunches overlapping to cover the base. Accents of red peppers, globe amaranth, bittersweet berries, and yarrow were pinned among the herbs. Some of the yarrow was left its natural yellow; other was dyed a soft orange with fabric dye.

RIGHT: A study in brown, this cone-and-nut wreath displays the intricate patterns supplied by nature, that master designer.

Gather cones soon after they fall from the tree or simply pluck them off. Test by squeezing: if the cone doesn't crumble, it's usable. Nuts are equally variable: buckeyes, acorns, hazelnuts, even peach pits.

Bake all nuts for 25 minutes at 200° F., and clip any stems from cones. For variety in color, cones can be soaked in a strong bleach solution and allowed to dry. To make the flowers, cut cones care-fully crosswise and remove any seeds that spoil the shape.

A piece of pegboard cut into a

LEFT : Essential to southwestern cuisine, large red ancho peppers make an arresting Christmas wreath in any part of the country. The base for this one is a wire ring wrapped in raffia, which provides both a strong base and a wide, flat surface for attaching materials. All materials are hot-glued on, the peppers first, then the accents: miniature corn, eucalyptus sprigs, cone flowers, nuts, and pods. A wired raffia bow adds a final splash of color.

BELOW : Regardless of what else is in the room, this dramatic wreath will capture attention. For one thing, everyone will want to know what on earth it's made of. The answer: sorghum cane tops.

The designer wired sorghum tops onto a 16-inch (40 cm.) straw base, with each bunch overlapping the wired stems of the previous one. With the base completely covered, she sprayed it with a clear acrylic sealer, adding gloss and resilience. The next step was to wire on the bow, made from four yards (3.7 m.) of wired ribbon, in a watered-silk pattern. Then she hot-glued Christmas balls around the wreath, and glued cedar sprigs in place. Finally, she shaped the long ribbon streamers and glued them into position.

LEFT: Materials become traditional if they work so well we refuse to stop using them. The holly, pine, boxwood, and nandina berries in this Christmas wreath welcome all who approach the house.

To prolong the greenery's freshness, the designer cut it into short lengths and immersed it in water overnight. The next day, he picked small bunches around the outside edge of a straw base, starting at what would become the focal point—the bottom—and working up one side to the top, then working up the opposite side. Then he covered the rest of the base with greenery, picked in bunches of nandina berries, and wired a generous red bow to the bottom.

ABOVE: Sprigs of Fraser fir define the outside of this wreath, with bright green ground pine circling the center. White yarrow and pearly everlasting, reddish brown chamaecyparis, sweet Annie, and blue-green oregano provide colorful accents. All materials are picked into a straw base.

LEFT: If you mean to have a cotton-picking Christmas, here's the way to start. Mist a grapevine wreath with flat white paint from a spray can. Then wrap the wreath with narrow gold-metallic ribbon, and attach a few branches of cedar and a gold bow with hot glue. While the glue gun is still hot, attach the cotton bolls—full ones, half-open ones, and empty ones (those brown, starlike shapes). Then glue on a few sumac heads for extra color.

BELOW: Two red corn husk flowers and a lush green bow provide the focal point of this wreath. Pine needle bases such as this one are widely available, and corn husk flowers appear in some craft shops and specialty stores. (To make your own flowers, see page 23.) Attach the flowers first, by twisting their wire stems around the base. Make six or seven bows with three loops on each side, and nestle them around the flowers, twisting the wires around the base to attach them. Continue adding bows until the wreath is as full as you like. Finally, wrap a ribbon around the base and attach it with hot-glue.

RIGHT: Corn husk flowers, German statice, and red velvet ribbon make a memorable wreath. First attach the flowers by twisting their wire stems around the vine base. If necessary, secure them with additional wire. The flowers should be just touching; they can be gently pulled apart later to accommodate a bow. (To make your own corn husk flowers, see page 23.) Next, make nine or 10 bows, tuck them around the flowers, and wire them to the base. Continue to add bows until the wreath looks full enough. Hot-glue a piece of ribbon to the wreath and wrap it around the base. Finally, hot-glue pieces of German statice among the bows and down the base.

This striking ivory wreath illustrates just how many different shades come under the heading "white." The designer wired sphagnum moss around a six-inch (15 cm.) wire ring, to provide a pale, natural base. She then wired artemisia around the base, using very lightweight wire. The rest of the materials were hot-glued on: strawflowers, globe amaranth, white yarrow, baby's breath, and pearly everlasting.

This small wreath could grace a cabinet front, a bedstead, or a dark-colored wall. It is shown wired to a green silk hatbox, where it seems to shimmer.

This jaunty wreath combines natural and faux materials, all hot-glued onto a grapevine base. The sprigs of cedar were attached first, followed by hydrangea blossoms. Then came a strand of pearl garland, available by the foot at craft shops; the designer wired one end to the base and looped it around the wreath, hot-gluing it at strategic points. Dried pink roses, pepperberries, common backyard moss, and long, thin stalks of leptrosporum add color and shape.

Large, lush, and full, this wreath still looks light enough to hang above a delicate mantle. The base consists of branches of fresh bay leaves wired to an eight-inch (20 cm.) wire ring. Gold sleigh bells are wired onto the base between the leaves, and flowers and herbs are hot-glued at random: zinnias, boneset, strawflowers, artemisia, and unidentified pink berries from the designer's backyard.

Neon-yellow lemons contrast nicely with dark magnolia leaves. A straw base works well for this kind of wreath. To make a similar one, first pin magnolia leaves around the front, using floral pins, making sure the leaves point outward. Then fill in the front of the wreath with pine, attaching it with pins, and pick clusters of boxwood between the magnolia leaves. Now for the lemons. Pierce each one end-to-end with a piece of heavy (18-gauge) wire, leaving several inches protruding from each end. Fold the wire ends straight back, and push them through the base, front to back, tucking the ends into back of the base. Hot-glue heads of red yarrow onto the greenery, and add a few cone flowers.

Because this fresh fruit wreath is heavy, the designer made a double base. She cut out a wreath-shaped piece of thin plywood and hammered medium-small nails through the wood, back to front, encircling the base and leaving the sharp nails projecting from the front side. Then she pushed blocks of dry foam onto the nails, producing a foam base backed with wood—which she then covered with Spanish moss.

Magnolia leaves picked around the outside and inside diameters form the basic wreath shape, and fruit supplies the decoration. The grapes are attached with U-shaped wires inserted over the stems at strategic locations. The apples and oranges are impaled on picks, whose pointed ends are inserted into the foam. Cinnamon sticks are picked and hot-glued around for accents.

LEFT: Glittering copper ribbon and matte green leaves—contrasting colors and surfaces make this table wreath an intriguing centerpiece. The designer covered the straw base with protea leaves, picking them at an angle so that they overlap well. She then taped plastic candle holders onto the base. Next came wispy plumosa fern, hot-glued between the leaves. She gave the wreath two bows: first a large one of copper-foil ribbon, then a smaller one on top. Finally, she hot-glued white parchment flowers around the bow and inserted the candles.

BELOW: Supported by a well-soaked ring of wet foam, the materials in this fresh table wreath will last throughout the Christmas season. Evergreens are inserted directly into the foam, and weak-stemmed English ivy is picked in. The tangerines are wired onto the base. (To wire the fruit, pierce it from side to side with a piece of heavy floral wire, leaving about two inches on each side. Bend the ends straight back, and insert them into the foam.) Hot-glue cinnamon sticks to the ends of picks and insert into the foam.

A white wreath on a dark door—what could be more striking? This bunnytail wreath would impress even the bunnies. To make it, you'll need white and red bunnytails, both available at craft shops. Wire the white bunnytails into full bunches, about four inches (10 cm.) wide and six inches (15 cm.) long. Then wire the bunches to a 24-inch (60 cm.) wreath base—either vine or wire will do—overlapping them so that the stems are covered. For a full, lush look, make sure to cover the inside and outside diameters, as well as the front. Wire together small bunches of red bunnytails, attach to picks, and insert them into the wreath at random.

Paint some tiny baskets gold (these are one inch wide and two inches high, or 2.5 by 5 cm.). Wire a pick to the back of each basket, and hot-glue a sprig of greenery inside, at the back. Glue dried roses, celosia, and globe amaranth inside each basket, to make miniature arrangements. Pick in the baskets around the wreath.

Form a bow from gold wired-net ribbon and wire it to the wreath, arranging the streamers around the wreath and wiring them into position.

The two window arrangements echo the wreath. The copper containers hang from ribbon and conceal bricks of foam. Each tiny, gold-painted basket holds a sprig of boxwood glued to the inside back, roses, and white ammobium blooms. Hook one end of a piece of wire through the bottom of the basket; the other end will be inserted into the foam.

Insert small branches of Scotch pine at the corners of the container. Then add lots of red bunnytails and a few white ones, some globe amaranth, and thistles. Insert the picked baskets and, toward the back, stems of rice grass. Tie a length of ribbon to the handles, and hang.

Arrangements

Materials and container echo each other in this coppery arrangement. A block of foam holds dried flowers and grasses, some common, some not (local crafts stores often carry surprising numbers of dried naturals).

Starting at the center back, insert stems of cinquefoil across the width of the container, spacing them evenly. Then add rows of natural bunnytails, peach rice grass, peach peppergrass, and baby's breath. Add peach statice sinuata in front, leaving a small space for the ornament. Attach a piece of wire to the top of the ornament, and insert it into the foam. Form a bow by wrapping wired metallic-copper ribbon around a candle, a dowel, or your finger; attach a wire, insert it into the foam, and position the streamers.

LEFT: Graceful lines and traditional Christmas colors characterize this striking arrangement. The designer began by cutting a piece of dry foam to fit a purchased pine-needle basket, and then covering the foam with deer moss. She attached slim red tapers to six-inch (15 cm.) picks with floral tape, and inserted them into the foam. Then came the vertical and horizonal cedar boughs, to establish the arrangement's basic shape, and the pine cones, attached to picks.

(Holes drilled in the cones made it easier to insert the picks.) Red rose hips and white rabbit tobacco added color, along with dried pomegranates cut in half and hot-glued to picks (one was hot-glued directly onto the front of the basket). An extra cone and a red bird were hot-glued to the bottom, and loops of watered-silk grosgrain ribbon picked in for a final touch.

BELOW: This Christmas mail-box is even busier than most.

Green velvet ribbons were hot-glued around the box, front and back, along with an alert-looking bird. Lined with plastic, the mail-box holds a water-soaked piece of wet floral foam, into which the designer inserted whatever greenery was at hand. A streamer of ivy was pulled up across the box and tucked under the bird, to keep his feet warm. Berries and twigs were inserted into the foam, and various nuts, cones, and acorns hot-glued in place.

Orchids and onions, eucalyptus and okra—if you're more interested in shapes and colors than in traditional categories, you'll combine odd things, often with arresting results.

Centered in the whitewashed market basket is a bowl containing wet floral foam and held in place by crumpled newspaper. First came a base of greenery: cedar, silver dollar eucalyptus, and variegated foliage. Then came the fruit. The bunch of red grapes was wired at the stem, then wired around a large pick. Large picks were inserted directly into the other produce—red onions, mushrooms, and okra— and then into the foam. Last came the flowers, inserted directly into the foam: giant white fujimums, a stalk of fleshy green leucodendron in the center, and elegant orchids.

The sweeping lines and subtle colors of this arrangement earn it a place at any table. A gold-painted basket lined with heavy plastic acts as a container, with a water-soaked piece of floral foam taped inside. The first materials used were three large pieces of cedar, inserted to form a triangle. Then dried pomegranates and step mushrooms were picked in, emphasizing the triangular shape. A lamé tube bow provides the focal point, with additional pomegranates, mushrooms, and gold-painted sweet gum balls clustered around it. Two 20-inch (50 cm.) mauve candles were taped to wooden picks and inserted slightly to the right of center, with boxwood and more cedar used to fill in around the accent pieces.

Full, heavy sorghum tops can produce a lush arrangement. For this one, the designer cut a piece of dry foam to fit a rustic basket, and covered it with moss. Since the sorghum tops were the heaviest materials, she inserted them first, establishing the basic shape of the arrangement. Then came common field thistles, followed by dried red and pink roses. Branches of lunaria (money plant) added round white leaves, and red eucalyptus added burgundy ones. The final touches were sprigs of baby's breath and a velvet bow.

LEFT: Nothing warms the heart (and the feet) like a roaring fire, and these pine cones will set even the stubbornest logs ablaze. Coated in paraffin and scented with cinnamon oil, they can be tossed in the fireplace, covered with kindling and "squaw wood," and lit with a match, adding their flames to the fire and their fragrance to the house. Packed in an attractive basket and bedecked with a bow, these fire starters make a perfect gift for friends who love a fire but hate to build one.

The ingredients include pine cones of various sizes, paraffin (available at most hardware stores and wherever canning supplies are sold), a double boiler, red crayons, and cinnamon oil (one teaspoon to two pounds of paraffin).

Cover your work table with newspaper. Remove the paper from the crayons, and break them into pieces. Melt the paraffin in a double boiler over hot water. *Do not melt paraffin directly on the burner or over an open flame. It may catch fire if you do.* Add pieces of red crayon until the wax is the desired color, then add the cinnamon oil.

Using tongs, dip the pine cones in the paraffin, and set them on the newspaper to dry. Allow the coated cones to dry, and then dip them again; repeat until cones are well covered. Allow the wax to dry completely.

Like all flammable materials, the cones should be stored a safe distance from the fire.

BELOW: The toys and goodies in these sleighs are all natural materials, wired into the spray-painted wicker sides. The white sleigh contains sprigs of holly and evergreen, peppers, cinnamon sticks, nuts, Christmas cherry, and prickly brown burrs. Riding in the red sleigh are sprigs of evergreen, statice, strawflower, peppers, cinnamon sticks, nuts, and Christmas cherry.

This three-foot (90 cm.) candy cane won't hurt your teeth or your waistline; it was cut from a two-inch-thick (5 cm.) sheet of foam. Natural materials picked in careful rows create the striped illusion.

A background of Fraser fir alternates with rows of red and then pink globe amaranth, tufted celosia, and bushy heads of sedum Autumn Joy. Hang this wall arrangement in a prominent place, and enjoy all those admiring comments.

Like most stockings, this one is filled with nice surprises. The base is a piece of two-inch-thick foam (5 cm.) cut into the proper shape. Sprigs of ground pine were picked in for greenery, with two or three sprigs per pick. Spilling out of the top are branches of Fraser fir, German statice, pink amaranth, celosia, yarrow, sumac heads, and statice sinuata in bright pink and purple.

LEFT: This woodsy arrangement looks as if it came out of someone's backyard. It did—and a small backyard, at that. A natural stick basket lined with heavy plastic holds a brick of wet floral foam, lying catty-cornered, back left to front right. Moss tucked around the foam hides it from view. Mushrooms on floral picks were inserted into the foam through the sides of the basket, and a few lichen-covered twigs hot-glued to the outside. Various greenery was then inserted into the foam—mountain laurel, white pine, holly, hemlock, and some variegated shrubbery no one could identify. Ivy streamers trail out the sides and encircle the handle. A few gold-spray-painted sorghum heads add body, some nameless red berries add color, and a perky little bird, hot-glued to the handle, adds cheer.

BELOW: This little basket (6-1/2 inches, or 16.25 cm., tall), frosted with a gold paint pen, holds a variety of unusual materials, all hot-glued to the inside: boneset, love-in-a-mist pods, globe amaranth, strawflowers, and gilded boxwood sprigs. Narrow ribbon is woven through the center of a length of net ribbon, which is glued to the handle. A bow made from 3/4-inch (1.9 cm.) wired ribbon, complete with streamers, graces the front.

ORNAMENTS

LEFT: The miniature baskets sold in every craft store make perfect Christmas tree ornaments. Just hot-glue small sprigs of dried materials inside. These contain yarrow, German statice, peppergrass, baby's breath, and globe amaranth. The handles are decorated with three narrow ribbons braided together and tied in a small bow at the center. Hot glue secures the ribbon in the center and on the sides.

TOP RIGHT: This elaborate ornament would be at home on the most formal tree. To make a similar one, you'll need about five feet (1.5 m.) of 1/8-inch (3 mm.) ribbon in one color, 10 feet (3 m.) in another color (divided in half), and a yard (90 cm.) of tiny glass beads, along with a basket and some dried flowers.

First braid a 16-inch (40 cm.) strip, using two strips of ribbon and one of beads; knot and glue the ends. Braid the remaining ribbon, and glue it to the basket as shown. Then glue the beads next to the braided ribbon. Glue the flowers and greenery into the basket: celosia, German statice, and eucalyptus leaves. Glue any loose beads in the center of the eucalyptus leaves, and glue braided bead-and-ribbon strips at the sides, allowing the extra to hang down the sides.

BOTTOM RIGHT: The designer used three kinds of ribbon on this gold-sprayed basket: net, plain, and wired. She wrapped three-inch (7.5 cm.) net ribbon around the basket and 1/8-inch (3 mm.) gold ribbon around the handle; both were hot-glued at the ends. Then she hot-glued baby's breath, rosebuds, strawflowers, globe amaranth, boxwood sprigs, and rose hips inside. Finally, she glued a small wired-ribbon bow to the handle.

For even dressier baskets, spray-paint them gold and wrap them in lace, securing it with hot glue, as this designer did. Because the dried materials are very delicate, she filled the baskets with wet-style floral foam and covered it with Spanish moss. She wired several fragrant star anise and inserted them into the foam, then added lavender, tansy, statice sinuata, caspia, pearly everlasting, artemisia, crested celosia, eucalyptus, and globe amaranth. Gold cord serves as hangers.

Touches of color warm the icy glitter of these icicles. Glued to the tops are tiny sprigs of asparagus fern, peppergrass, German statice, pepperberries, celosia, strawflowers, and an occasional rose. Ribbons serve as hangers.

Elongated ornaments are interesting contrasts to the usual round shapes that bedeck the tree. Glued to the blown-glass ornament at left are silver king artemisia, sprigs of blue salvia, and delphinium blooms. The ornament at right boasts German statice, tiny pink peppergrass, strawflowers, pepperberries, celosia, and globe amaranth. Each is topped with a ribbon that serves as a hanger.

Blown-glass bells cascading down the tree add both color and sound; they really do ring when a draft moves through the room. Hot-glued on top are German statice, pepperberries, celosia, peppergrass, and globe amaranth. Loops of ribbon make graceful hangers.

LEFT: Ordinary glass Christmas balls can become distinctive ornaments with natural materials hot-glued to the outside and a bright bow tied to the hanger. A well-shaped leaf of dusty miller adorns the silver ball at far left, topped with a sprig of blue salvia and a delphinium bloom. Silver ribbon ties it all together. The blown glass ornament at left also holds dusty miller, topped with artemisia and delphinium. The wired blue ribbon makes an especially effective bow.

The red and white bouquet in the inset photo consists of German statice, globe amaranth, and celosia.

TOP RIGHT: On these ornaments, dusty miller leaves support dainty peppergrass, topped with pepperberries and strawflowers. The materials at far right also include dusty miller, peppergrass, and strawflowers, but add celosia and a pink rose on top.

BOTTOM RIGHT: Glass balls filled with potpourri add scent to the tree. Remove the metal hook and wire from the top of the ornament, fill the ball about a third full of potpourri, and reattach hook to top, using a drop of quick glue. Run a piece of thin floral wire through a piece of lace, gathering it, and attach it to the top. Add a bow and hanger, and top bow with globe amaranth.

Miniature vine wreaths make versatile bases. You can buy them ready-made or make your own: just shape the vines into wreaths and tie or wire together. Then select herbs and everlastings in complementary colors and hot-glue them around the wreath in sequence.

Mountain mint was the first herb applied to these wreaths; the leaves cover the bases, overlapping in the same direction. Accent materials add color and shape: lavender, nigella, straw-flowers, pearly everlasting, globe amaranth, crested celosia, and artemisia.

These wreath bases are wire and lace. To make one, thread a piece of floral wire though a piece of lace 15 inches (37.5 cm.) long and four inches (10 cm.) wide, gathering it by going in and out of the holes until you've formed a seven-inch (17.5 cm) circle. Tie the wire together, and add a ribbon loop as a hanger. Very carefully dot hot glue along the wire, fold the lace over, and hold until dry, doubling it for a fluffy effect. Hot-glue mountain mint leaves around the inside of the lace circle, and then hot-glue on your remaining herbs and flowers: sweet Annie for fragrance, crested celosia, globe amaranth, strawflowers, and pearly everlasting.

Strawberry corn is an ornamental with cobs about two inches (5 cm.) long. Available as seed corn for the home garden or as full-grown cobs in the fall, strawberry corn is a perfect shape and color for a Christmas ornament.

This cob was shorn of its husks, sprayed with a glossy acrylic coating, and allowed to dry. Five holly leaves painted gold (either paint pen or spray can would work) were hot-glued on top, along with a loop of gold wire with attached stars, to serve as a hanger. Finally, a small sprig of pepperberries was hot-glued on top.

The corn husks were left on this cob of strawberry corn, becoming essential parts of the design. After soaking for a few minutes in warm water, the brittle husks became pliable enough to work with. When dry, they were gilded with a paintbrush barely dipped in gold paint.

A loop of ribbon hot-glued to the center of the cob serves as a hanger. Most of the husk tips were bent forward and glued onto the corn, forming loops; two were left extended. Eucalyptus leaves were overlapped around the top of the cob, and celosia and globe amaranth filled in the spaces created by the loops. The tip of a eucalyptus branch was glued to the bottom of the ornament, to help balance it visually, and the ornament sprayed with a glossy acrylic finish.

LEFT: Red, white, and gold—these joyous colors are reflected in natural materials. The husks on the strawberry corn were soaked for a few minutes, to make them pliable, then trimmed with scissors into shorter and narrower shapes. When they were almost dry, they were bent into interesting shapes, then allowed to dry completely. With the cob covered in plastic wrap, for protection, the husks were spray-painted gold, top and bottom. A piece of gold cord was hot-glued on as a hanger. Then came the flowers. Glue was applied to the ends of white ammobium blossoms, and the flowers placed at random. Finally, the cob was sprayed with clear acrylic finish.

RIGHT: This zippy ornament consists of kernels of Indian corn glued onto a foam ball. A "hairpin" made of floral wire, looped and inserted into the ball, forms the hanger, and plaid ribbon in complementary colors provides a finishing touch.

LEFT: Pomanders are time-hon-ored Christmas decorations, and for excellent reason. They're fra-grant, pretty, and made from everyday materials. Pierce a whole fresh orange all over with a nail, and insert whole cloves into the holes. (The nail spares fingers and cloves.) Let the pomander dry until it feels almost weightless, compared to its former hefty self. Drying takes about six hours in a dehydrator and several days in a dry, cool place. Attach a ribbon as if wrapping a package and tie a knot on top, leaving the ends long enough to make a hanger. Hot-glue three bay leaves around the knot and three caspia on top. Then add one-inch (2.5 cm.) cin-namon sticks, strawflowers, and whole star anise. Finish with three globe amaranth, glued as close to the ribbon as possible. Tie the rib-bon ends together as a hanger.

RIGHT: Both evergreen and cinnamon have distinctive Christ-mas scents. Together, they can infuse an entire house with holi-day spirit.

Each of these fragrant orna-ments consists of a purchased cin-namon broom decorated with herbs and flowers. A small bunch of naturals was wired together with fine-gauge floral wire, spread out into a fan shape to match the broom, and then wired onto the neck of the broom.

The brilliant broom at right supports magenta globe amaranth and small white snowflake flowers on a bed of garden thyme and sil-ver king artemisia. The broom in the inset photo is decorated with silver king artemisia and yarrow, both natural yellow and dyed orange with fabric dye.

Fragrant spice balls become lovely tree decorations when dried leaves and flowers are added. A piece of lace was folded accordion-style, wired in a circle, and hot-glued to the top of the ball. Then leaves and flowers were hot-glued to the lace. While the lace isn't a prominent feature of the ornament, it does provide an attractive base.

LEFT: The ornament at top is decorated with silver-green lamb's ears, yellow tansy, fuzzy stillingia, and a rosebud. The lower spice ball sports peppermint leaves and flowers, and colorful globe amaranth.

BELOW: The left and center spice balls are enlivened with German statice, loops of metallic ribbon, and a prominent rose. The ball at right adds silver germander leaves to the mix.

Making Spice Balls

These small pomanders are really highly spiced applesauce. To make them, drain a jar of applesauce for about 30 minutes. In a medium mixing bowl, combine ground cinnamon, cloves, mace, and nutmeg in equal amounts. Gradually add drained applesauce to the spices until the mixture has the consistency of stiff cookie dough. Shape the dough into balls, place them on waxed paper, and allow to dry for three weeks (longer in humid weather). Decorate the spice balls with ribbons, lace, and dried materials.

LEFT: Most of us have spent a cozy December evening stringing popcorn and cranberries for the Christmas tree. Dried flowers—in this case, globe amaranth—can be strung in exactly the same way for a brilliant and unusual garland. Remove the stems but keep the leaves that are inclined to remain. Then thread a large needle with thin monofilament (fishing line) or heavy thread, and string the flowers. When the garland is the length you want (or when you run out of flowers), tie off both ends, and drape the garland through the branches.

RIGHT: Scatter small nosegays of dried flowers through the branches of your tree, for a pretty, light-hearted effect. Just wrap some floral wire about the stems, leaving enough excess wire to form a loop at the bottom; the loop will wrap around the tree branch, holding the nosegay in place. Then wrap the stems with floral tape, to create a smooth, firm handle.

The nosegay on top consists of sage, statice sinuata, German statice, and magenta globe amaranth. The one at center left boasts red and white strawflowers, pearly everlasting, and red and pink amaranth. At center right is a nosegay of red celosia, white statice sinuata, and pink and white amaranth. The simple white ornament at bottom contains pearly everlasting, silver king artemisia, and white amaranth.

LEFT: If you've been wondering what to do with the seashells you gathered last summer, here's one solution. Loosely fold a length of ribbon in half and hot-glue it to the back of the shell, so that a loop about an inch (2.5 cm.) long shows on top and tails of about two inches (5 cm.) show on the bottom. Hot-glue herbs and flowers to the front side: mint leaves in a triangle, overlaid with caspia, then lavender, celosia, strawflowers, and tiny globe amaranth.

RIGHT: They may look elaborate, but these miniature tussie mussies are simply tiny bouquets in small paper-doily cuffs, available at most crafts stores. Start by gluing shapely green leaves (these are mint) around the base. Then make a small bouquet of dried flowers and herbs, wrapping the stems together with floral tape, positioning the flowers on the outside lower than those in the center. (Don't let the bouquet get too wide to fit into the cuff.) Cut the stems to two or three inches (5 to 7.5 cm.), and insert the stems into the cuff. Rewrap with tape to secure cuff. Add a bow of gold curling-paper ribbon and a hanger of gold elastic cord.

The bouquets shown include roses, sweet Annie, lavender, statice sinuata, pearly everlasting, and globe amaranth.

LEFT: Scented geranium leaves, catnip flowers, roses, lavender, straw-flowers, globe amaranth, celosia, statice sinuata, artemisia—all grace this Victorian ornament. If your favorite craft store doesn't stock paper cones rimmed with lace, cut a paper disc, make a cut from the outside edge to the center, and glue the cone together. Snip off the point and glue a piece of lace around the top. Fold two eight-inch (20 cm.) pieces of ribbon in half, wire them in the center, and insert them through the hole at the bottom, leaving enough inside the cone to hot-glue in place. Hot-glue a ribbon hanger to the rim, a piece of floral foam inside the cone, and green forest moss over it. Working from the perimeter to the center and leaving a rim of moss showing, hot-glue herbs and flowers on the moss. Add a small dove.

TOP: "What on earth is *that?*" will break the ice rather well at your Christmas open house—a good reason to deck your tree with exotic lotus pods, available in the "drieds" section of the local craft store. Spray-paint the pod gold, and drill a hole into the stalk end. Fold a length of gold cord in half and hot-glue both ends in the hole, to serve as a hanger. Then hot-glue on herbs, flowers and a small bird.

BOTTOM: According to Scandinavian legend, each bird on your Christmas tree will bring one year of good luck. Start your aviary with a bluebird nesting in potpourri. Run a wire up through the bottom of a purchased nest and back out again, to wrap around a tree branch. Apply hot glue to the inside of the nest and spread with potpourri. Install the bird with hot glue, and surround him or her with herbs and flowers.

Each of these intricate ornaments is a circle of red cardboard with seeds arranged in an interesting pattern, attached with white craft glue. At left, sea oats form a backdrop for white squash seeds, brown persimmon seeds, cantaloupe seeds dyed green, and a hemlock cone. The center ornament includes sea oats, corn kernels, hemlock cones, cantaloupe seeds dyed blue, and a eucalyptus pod. At right, the sea oats are topped with cantaloupe seeds dyed red, Job's tears, Japanese watermelon seeds, and a small cone cup.

To make a double ornament that can be displayed from both sides, make two and glue them back to back.

The bells of Christmas are ringing! To make these bright ornaments, cut a bell shape from cardboard and from two pieces of felt. Glue the three together, using white craft glue, with the cardboard in the middle to add stiffness. Then glue on some seeds or small cones.

The red bell is decorated with squash seeds and a small acorn in the center. The blue bell adds some variegated Japanese watermelon seeds. On the green bell are sea oats, hemlock cones, cantaloupe seeds dyed red, and a small acorn in the center.

How to Dye Seeds
Wash any pulp from the seeds, and allow them to dry thoroughly. Spread them out on a baking sheet and set them in a sunny place or in a warm oven until they are thoroughly dry.

Combine one tablespoon of ordinary fabric dye, two cups of water, and a little salt in an enamel pan. For a deeper color, add more dye. Boil the seeds until you like the color, then set them aside to dry.

LEFT: Sweet or hot, red peppers are colorful enough to hang on the tree. The large ancho peppers are tied by their stems with bright red raffia and decked out in nuts, cones and eucalyptus—all hot-glued in place. Bright raffia bows add pizzazz.

The small rings were made by threading fruit and nuts onto a piece of medium-gauge floral wire, then forming the wire into a circle and hooking the ends around each other, so that the circle stays closed. The upper ornament holds nuts, hot peppers, and Christmas cherries. The lower one adds two orange calendula blossoms.

TOP RIGHT: Pine cones can be had for the picking. Make sure the cones are firm, then hot-glue the ends of a red velvet ribbon to the underside of a couple of the cone's seeds. Finally, hot-glue your materials in place: cedar, rose hips, and a bright red bow.

BOTTOM RIGHT: Star-shaped cotton bolls can be decorated as rustic-looking ornaments. The top one has a seed "daisy" with a gumball center and petals made from cherry pits and pumpkin seeds. The bottom boll is dressed with a small gumball and hemlock cones. Both hang from red velvet ribbons hot-glued in place.

Christmas in the kitchen doesn't have to stop with once-a-year cookies and cranberries. Everyday garlic, that fragrant herb we couldn't do without, deserves a little finery too. Hot-glue some rosemary sprigs and scarlet globe amaranth among the bulbs of a garlic swag, attach a bow made from wired-cord ribbon, and hang the swag where you can admire it—and where it will keep the Christmas vampires at bay.

LEFT: This six-foot (1.8 m.) garland is just the right length to dress up a plain white door. It displays four different shades of green because it's made from four different evergreens: hemlock, white pine, blue juniper, and evergreen japonica. Rabbit tobacco lightens the garland with touches of white. The ingredients were wired separately into bundles with fine-gauge floral wire, and the bundles wired to a spine of heavy-gauge wire. A six-foot garland requires about 40 sprigs of each evergreen and as many bundles of flowers as you like.

RIGHT: There's nothing complex about this festive swag: branches of evergreens and holly arranged in a fan shape and wired together at the top, with a red velvet bow wired on for color. For easier hanging, make a loop of wire and attach it before adding the bow.

These swags are simply horizontal bouquets held together with wire and hot glue. The base of the green and red swag is a large bunch of eucalyptus and silver king artemisia, wired together in the middle. Pepperberries and cranberry celosia are hot-glued to the base, and a paper bow is wired to the center.

The smaller pink swag has a base of silver king artemisia, wired in the center, with other materials hot-glued on top: long pink larkspur, crested celosia, hydrangea, and strawflowers. A bow of pink grosgrain ribbon ties the colors together.

The materials for this festive garland are as simple as the technique used to make it. A length of green jute cord (the type used in macrame) was stretched taut between two chair backs, at a comfortable working height. Then bunches of pine and gypsophila (baby's breath) were alternately tied to the cord with flexible, spool-type floral wire, each bunch overlapping the previous one. Bright plaid bows were wired to the ends.

Many craft stores carry wheat sheaves that are wired, fumigated, and ready for decorating. If you gather wheat from the fields, zap it for a few seconds in the microwave or fumigate it, to get rid of bugs. Then shape it into a sheaf and wire it together around the middle. Trim off some of the wheat heads on one side, so that the swag will hang flat against the wall. (Save the trimmings.) Make six bows with three loops on each side (you don't need a center loop), wire each in the center, and wire the bows tightly to the sheaf. Hot-glue the trimmed wheat heads randomly among the ribbons. If you hang your sheaf outside, like the one in the inset photo, prepare to fend off hungry birds.

You can dress up a cabinet of collectibles with Christmas candles, fresh fruit, and a graceful garland. Or, in this case, three garlands: cedar, cranberry, and ivy. You'll need small nails on the top of the cabinet—in the center and at both corners—to hold the garland, or some other means of attachment.

First make a cedar garland. Wire small bunches of cedar along a piece of five-ply jute cord, overlapping the bunches for fullness and to conceal the previous wired ends.

Now string very fresh cranberries on lengths of substantial thread, with buttons at the beginning and end to keep the cranberries in place.

Finally, wire together lengths of ivy to make a garland. Twist the ivy and berry garlands around each other, and tie with string every 12 inches (30 cm.) or so.

Wire the cedar garland to the center nail, then to the two outer ones, allowing it to droop gracefully in between. Wire the berry-ivy garland to the center nail and then to the outer ones, allowing it to drape down the sides of the cabinet.

Form a bow, wire it to the center nail, arrange the streamers the way you want them, and wire into position. Wire on some holly leaves, novelty packages, sumac heads, or anything else you have around that would look good. Finally, arrange cedar branches, fruit, and candles at the base.

LEFT: This handsome door swag is too heavy to rely on foam alone for support. The designer hot-glued a long rectangle of two-inch-thick green Styrofoam (5 cm.) to a sturdy board; the foam provided a means of anchoring the greenery, and the board supplied the necessary backing.

After he built the support, the designer secured a brass trumpet to the foam with an electrical conduit clamp. Branches of Fraser fir, picked into the foam, established the general shape. Then he filled in the center with short pieces of fir, eucalyptus, and boxwood. Dried pomegranates, cones, celosia, and wheat, picked in bunches, add interesting detail, along with a bow and streamers of Hunter green grosgrain ribbon.

A single cinnamon broom can fill a house—a large house—with the sweet, spicy scent that says Christmas. Widely available, the brooms can be decorated with just about anything. For this one, the designer wired on some cattails first and some corn husk flowers second, twisting the flower stems through the broom and adding more wire in back. (To make the flowers, see page 23.) She then made six plaid bows with three loops on each side and wired them over the cattails and around the flowers.

BELOW: For this glitzy swag, the designer spray-painted two bunches of wheat a bright silver, laid them end-to-end, and wired them together by their stems. After hot-gluing on some sprigs of peppergrass, she covered the wire with ribbon, then hot-glued a bow to the front and a pink-painted sea grape leaf to the back.

RIGHT: Old hand tools are often pleasing to the eye. With more work to do than time to do it in, our ancestors honed and shaped and experimented, searching for the most efficient design, the most muscle-sparing shape. As often as not, efficiency and grace went together. The owner of this antique sickle wired a period-looking bow to it, hot-glued pine and eucalyptus sprigs under the bow, hot-glued on some dried caspia, and hung the attention-getting swag on the wall.

LEFT: A partridge in a pear tree can perch happily on buffet table or bookcase. Inside the brass container, a green plastic pot full of plaster of Paris holds a tree branch upright and steady. The top of the plaster is spray-painted moss green, for camouflage. A foam cone, hot-glued to the top of the "trunk," holds sprigs of boxwood inserted at a downward slope. (In this case, the designer began at the top and continued downward to the base.) Strong-stemmed bosc pears are wired to three-inch (7.5 cm.) picks and inserted into the foam, and a purchased partridge roosts on top.

THIS PAGE: Flat but emphatically three-dimensional, this two-foot-tall (60 cm.) wall tree supplies that indispensable Christmas-tree fragrance. The base is a sheet of two-inch-thick (5 cm.) plastic foam cut in a tree shape. Pieces of Fraser fir are inserted at a sharp, downward-sloping angle, to mimic tree branches. Sumac heads and sprigs of German statice, both picked into the base, provide the red and white decorations.

A curly willow "trunk" makes this topiary as graceful as it is festive. After gluing dry foam into a clay pot and covering the foam with moss, the designer inserted the willow branches, their stems cut at a sharp angle for easier insertion. She then placed a foam ball in the top branches, tied the branches around the ball, and covered it with moss. Architecture completed, she turned to decorating. At top and bottom she picked evergreens, holly, and dried sweet Annie into the foam. Next she glued a length of ribbon to the top, wound it down to the bottom, and ended with a ribbon loop. Finally, she hot-glued on the apples, birds, and a bird's nest—which she also trimmed for Christmas.

This graceful topiary is simpler than it looks. To make a similar one, arrange a double handful of cattails around a sturdy dowel, then wire them in the middle and at the bottom. Wire on the upper bow, and cover its wire (and the one binding the cattails) with ribbon. Hot-glue pieces of fungus and sponge mushrooms to the base, glue on the lower bow, and tuck in some strands of Spanish moss. Finally, hot-glue sprigs of boxwood around the bows.

A grapevine tree is a woodsy base for materials straight from the forest. (For instructions on making one, see page 20.) This tree is lit with 35 clear mini-lights; the cord spirals down the inside of the tree, with the bulbs pulled through to the outside. A circle of plastic foam covered with sheet moss sits inside the bottom of the tree and holds two small pots of English ivy, whose streamers have been pulled out through the vines. Other materials are hot-glued directly onto the tree: dried mushrooms and lichens, deer moss, rabbit tobacco, dried sweetheart roses, hemlock cones, protea buds, and faux blackberries. Three feet (90 cm.) of gold bullion—a spiderweb-like gold thread—wraps around the tree as a garland.

Fresh carnations add color and a spicy scent to this tabletop tree. To build a similar one, stand a block of wet floral foam on end in the middle of a low serving dish (this one is 14 inches, or 35 cm., across), and tape the foam to the dish. Insert sprigs of boxwood, forming a tree shape. Then insert red sumac heads, spacing them equally around the tree, using the larger ones at the bottom. Add miniature pink carnations, again distributing them evenly. Then pick in German statice, white pine cone "roses" (cones cut in half), and gold-painted gumballs from a sweet gum tree. Water the tree daily, pouring water gently on top of the foam.

LEFT: This tree could not be simpler. Just trim a live, upright rosemary plant into a Christmas tree shape, and decorate it. This one is decorated with a miniature garland, tiny ornaments hung from gold thread, and stemless globe amaranth placed in the branches.

RIGHT: This shaggy little tree will endear itself to children visiting for the holidays. Put it in the guest bedroom you've assigned to the kids. A 12-inch (30 cm.) foam cone supports overlapping sprigs of white pine that have been inserted at an angle, allowing the needles to slope downward, like those of a real tree. A few sprigs were then inserted upright, at the top. The "ornaments" consist of statice, yarrow, sweet Annie, ambrosia, and silver king artemisia.

LEFT: Some years, December seems to be six weeks long, with enough time for everything we want to do. Other years, December has six days—max. If this is one of your short seasons, consider the advantages of an artificial tabletop tree. The base is ready-made, requiring at most a little trimming of extra-long branches. With enough natural materials, no one will ever know what it's like deep down.

This tree boasts a garland of blue larkspur glued end-to-end and spiraled down the tree. Gypsophila has been randomly scattered among the branches (a dab of hot glue on the cut stem holds each in place). Blue salvia hangs from the tips of the branches, held firmly by hot glue. Hot-glued globe amaranth blossoms cover the salvia ends and enliven other branches as well. A bow of wired ribbon tops the tree.

RIGHT: The contrasting colors in this free-standing tree are all supplied by natural materials. Ground pine and German statice contribute the green and white. Red is provided by celosia, purple by sage blossoms, and magenta by globe amaranth. All are picked into a 12-inch (30 cm.) foam cone.

The trees on both these pages started off green and artificial. On this page, a garland of naturals steals the show. To create a similar effect, twist Spanish moss into a "rope" and spiral it up the tree. Then, starting at the bottom, hot-glue flowers to the moss—in this case, roses, hydrangea, pearly everlasting, larkspur, celosia, peppergrass, strawflowers, statice, pepperberries, and globe amaranth. Cover the wooden stand with a piece of lace and a bow, and set another bow on top, with a small cluster of flowers hot-glued in the center.

Artemisia and German statice
turned this faux green tree into a
naturally pink-and-white one. The
designer inserted small branches
of both plants all over the tree,
cementing them in place with hot
glue. Decorative accents include
small blown glass balls, larkspur,
pearly everlasting, peppergrass,
celosia, and strawflowers. A small
bow with a rosebud in the center
tops the tree, and gathered lace
trim finishes the bottom.

PACKAGES

LEFT: The recipient of this gift will be at least as pleased by the decoration as by what's inside. The rich-looking paper has color enough, so the designer focused on scent and texture instead. Fir sprigs and boxwood hot-glued to the paper form a dark base, with pine cones and peppergrass glued on top.

BELOW: The deep green paper is a perfect backdrop for pale flowers and dark cones. Hot-glued to the paper in a cresent shape are pine cones, cone flowers (made by cutting the cones in half), German statice, pearly everlasting, and white strawflowers. One cone is lightly dusted with white spray paint.

LEFT: One of the best trends in gift-wrapping is the appearance of festive tote bags. They range in size from substantial to minuscule, ready to hold a VCR or a single truffle. This one is even more attractive than most. A corsage made of dried roses, pink-dyed peppergrass, sprays of pepperberries, and sprigs of boxwood is hot-glued to the bag.

BELOW: Wrapped in pink moiré paper, this elegant package will shine under the tree. A silver bow forms the center of the decoration, with materials hot-glued on each side: artemisia, dusty miller, celosia, dyed German statice, dyed peppergrass, and bunches of della robia grapes.

LEFT: This pink metallic bow is wired and ready to turn a mundane package into an occasion. The bow requires four feet (1.2 m.) of 1-1/2"-wide (3.75 cm.) ribbon. Leaving one tail 11 inches (27.5 cm) long and the other 19 inches (47.5 cm.) long, form a bow with six loops (three on each side) and wire it in the center, after pulling the tails into place. Leave enough wire to attach to a package's ribbon. Cut a disc of clear, lightweight plastic (check the kitchen) and glue it to the front of the bow, to serve as a base for the naturals. Working from the outside to the center, hot-glue the herbs and flowers onto the plastic disc: bay leaves, caspia, yarrow, lavender, statice, celosia, thistle, globe amaranth, and strawflowers.

CENTER: The square red package is decorated with pine cones, cinnamon sticks, star anise, and boxwood, hot-glued to the paper.

RIGHT: The elongated blooms of rattail celosia are the attention-getters on this small package. Also hot-glued to the pink moiré paper are boxwood, dyed peppergrass, and della robia fruit.

Treasures for the
CHRISTMAS TREE

Oh, Christmas Tree!

A Christmas tree is one of the best ideas anyone ever had. It sits joyfully in our winter-bound houses, green in a gray month, alive in the dead of winter, gleaming with light and color in a twilight season. Its sharp scent freshens our shuttered rooms, and underneath it are presents, small tokens of love.

Making ornaments for such a well-loved visitor is a pleasure.

Sometimes "making" ornaments really means gathering them: finding a perfect lichen on a tree outside that will look splendid on the tree inside. Sometimes "making" means exactly that—using a few simple tools and readily available materials to create an ornament from scratch.

The ornaments in this book use a variety of materials and cover a wide range of moods and tastes. There are ornaments made from flowers and herbs. Others are fashioned from gourds, pinecones and pine needles, cornhusks, wheat, and straw. A few are made from foodstuffs. Others started out as scraps of fabric, ribbon, yarn, or string; some of these must be sewn, but most rely on fabric glue. Finally, there's a chapter on all that glitters—craft gems, minerals, hot glitter glue, foil, mylar, and plastic.

Scattered through the book are ideas for decorating miniature Christmas trees. Not every room needs a six-foot evergreen, but every room rejoices in a tiny tree. Miniature trees allow you to deck *all* the halls. (They also make welcome gifts).

When we make our own ornaments, we join centuries of tradition. We've been trimming the tree for a long, long time.

The Dark Night of the Solstice

From the beginning of recorded history, human beings have staged midwinter festivals. The occasion was the winter solstice, which we seem to have identified in our infancy, when the only astronomical instruments were eyesight and memory. Occurring on December 21, the solstice marks the longest night and the shortest day of the year in the northern hemisphere. From the middle of June until the middle of December, as the days became ever briefer and the nights ever longer, we shivered in ancient dread that the pattern was fixed, that we were on a relentless descent into the cold and the dark.

The solstice was the turning point. When we knew almost nothing else, we knew that after December 21 the days would grow longer and the nights shorter, the darkness would recede and the life-giving, soul-restoring light return.

Now that's a reason for a party.

Oh, Solstice Tree!

For at least 4,000 years, trees, especially evergreen trees, have been part of solstice celebrations. In Mesopotamia a 12-day festival encompassed the six days before and the six days after the solstice. The high point was a mock battle between the mythical Sun King and the forces of darkness. The Sun King won every year. As part of the general rejoicing, trees—the soldiers of the sun—were decorated and then burned.

The ancient Greeks staged a midwinter festival in honor of Zeus, draping evergreens and other trees with garlands of flowers and herbs. The Romans celebrated the Feast of the Unconquered Sun, which they called Saturnalia in honor of the god Saturn, and it was such a good party—feasting, gift giving, storytelling, and general revelry—that *saturnalia* remains a synonym for "orgy." During the season, private houses and public buildings were graced with evergreen trees and boughs, hung with candles, berries, and small trinkets that were eventually taken down and given as gifts.

In northern Europe, evergreens were even more central to solstice celebrations. The ancient Celts of Britain, Ireland, and France decorated evergreens and oaks with apples and mistletoe, as did the Teutons of Germany and Scandinavia. Norsemen simply dug the trees up, brought them inside, and burned circles of candles around the bases. They also burned an especially long-lasting log in honor of the god Yolnir, the light bearer—hence "Yule" log.

Solstice's End

Early Roman Christians did not celebrate Jesus's birth, even after Christianity became the established religion of the Roman empire in the fourth century. Never ones to turn down a good time, however, the Romans did continue to celebrate Saturnalia.

Troubled by these echoes of paganism, the church proclaimed December 25 to be the birth date of Jesus. Thus midwinter festivals became, not pagan occasions, but a time of Christian rejoicing.

Many solstice customs were incorporated directly into Christmas: feasting, gift giving, storytelling (carols, for example), and the lighting of fires and candles. When it came to evergreens, however, the church drew the line. Intimately identified with centuries of paganism, evergreens were strictly forbidden.

The ban was hard to enforce, especially in Northern Europe, where evergreens were abundant and especially revered. Ultimately, the church found a place for Christmas greenery.

Oh, Tannenbaum!

Legends about the origin of the Christmas tree abound. While they differ widely in the people and events they recount, most mention Germany as the place of origin. Happily enough, that's also where the historical evidence places it.

The ancestor of the Christmas tree probably appeared in medieval Paradise plays in Germany. Faced with an illiterate populace, the church enlisted actors to portray the Christian story in the public square. Every year on December 24, actors staged the fall of Adam and Eve and the redemption of Christ. The only stage prop was a tree hung with apples, representing the tree of knowledge in the Garden of Eden. (The church put a halt to the plays when actors began to spice up the dialogue with overblown speeches and ribald jokes.)

The earliest recorded Christmas trees appeared in Germany in the 16th century. By the 17th century travelers were reporting that some German parlors boasted fir trees decorated with paper roses, apples, wafers, gold foil, and sugar sweets. By the 18th century, visitors were describing a small tree for each child in the family, with presents of new clothing, dolls, and candy underneath.

Germans emigres carried the custom to the rest of the Christian world. Prince Albert, husband and consort of Queen Victoria and a German by birth, introduced the Christmas tree into the British royal household, and from there it was a short step to the rest of the kingdom. German teachers and professors in the United States set up Christmas trees for their children and helped to popularize the custom in America.

An old custom, a joyous custom, a custom that bridges nations and even, in the broadest sense, religions—the Christmas tree remains the centerpiece of our midwinter celebrations.

Tips and Techniques

To hang happily from the branches of your evergreen, an ornament needs to meet only a few requirements.

Size. Ornaments need to be in scale with the tree they decorate. Even the most gorgeously carved basketball gourd will look preposterous on anything except a 60-foot Douglas fir, and a thimble-sized ornament may look lost on a full-size tree. Consider how big your tree will be and design accordingly.

Weight. Evergreens have very flexible branches that bend under the weight of heavy snow and heavy ornaments. It takes very few ounces to make a branch as droopy as the post-Christmas blues.

Visibility. If you'd rather sell your grandmother into slavery than put up a Christmas tree that isn't green, avoid ornaments that use a lot of foliage or that are simply green. They'll disappear into the tree. If you have a white tree, perhaps one that's generously covered with artificial snow, greenery will show up nicely.

Density. While it's a matter of personal preference, many people think that a tree looks best when it's thoroughly decorated—when there are lots of decorations per square foot. Feel free to combine handcrafted ornaments with purchased ones and to fill in with additional materials (see "Fillers" below).

Tools and Materials

Making the ornaments in this book requires very few tools—a craft knife here, a pair of pliers there. Mostly you'll need to attach things to each other.

Adhesives are essential, and there are lots of good ones on the market—white craft glue, tacky glue, fabric glue, epoxy, and the venerable glue gun. (If you haven't noticed that glue sticks for glue guns now come in a variety of colors, with or without glitter, let us be the first to pass on the news.) The directions for each project suggest the adhesives that will work best.

Wire is a fine means of attachment—flexible green floral wire, available in just about every craft department, and the brass wire used in jewelry making and other crafts, available in most craft stores.

Floral tape—brown or green, depending on the materials—is also useful; it binds delicate materials without damaging them.

Base Balls

When you set out to make your own Christmas balls, you can choose from two widely available bases to support your materials. Both work well.

Polystyrene foam balls come in sizes ranging from huge to tiny. Lightweight, versatile, and invaluable, they have only two drawbacks. Hot glue melts them, requiring the use of a low-melt glue gun, and since they have nothing to attach a loop of ribbon to, some kind of hanger has to be constructed.

Equally useful are the inexpensive ornaments variously described as "satin" (they aren't) or "silk" (they aren't that, either). Wound with shiny thread, these balls are lightweight and inexpensive. They accept glue well, including hot glue, and they come with a built-in metal ring that's a fine place to attach a hanger.

Hangers

Functional as they are, those galvanized metal hangers we all grew up with don't do much for a handsome ornament. A simple loop of narrow ribbon in a complementary color makes an enormous difference in an ornament's attractiveness. Also useful are embroidery floss, dyed suede thong, and woven metallic cord.

Fillers

If you don't have the time or the inclination to make enough ornaments to fully decorate a tree, consider adding fillers—materials you can add to the tree that look terrific and require virtually no work.

Dried flowers look spectacular on a tree. Wire the stems into small bundles, then wire the bundles to the tree. Or, assuming a pet- and child-free house, just tuck the flowers among the branches. White baby's-breath is particularly versatile, but other, more unusual flowers, such as dried hydrangeas, can be striking.

Garlands frame ornaments beautifully, and a variety of materials can be draped around the tree—ribbon, grapevine, raffia, even the classic popcorn and cranberry. A "garland" of well-placed dried flowers encircling the tree can be wonderful.

Bows are fine fillers, especially considering the variety of ribbons to choose from: velvet, paper, mesh, net, cellophane, metallic, printed.

Packages—quick, easy, and broadly defined—can add a note of fun: popcorn or candy tied up in colored cellophane and hung on the tree, satin ornaments tied up in netting. Wrap tiny boxes in Christmasy giftwrap and hang them on the tree.

Transferring Patterns

Most of the patterns in this book are so simple that you probably won't bother to transfer them. Even those of us who are drawing-impaired can sketch a star or a heart or a hobby horse.

If you prefer to transfer the pattern directly, the simplest method is to find a photocopy machine. If the pattern is shown full size, simply photocopy it and cut it out. When half the pattern is shown, position it carefully as you photocopy it, leaving enough room on the photocopied page for the half not pictured. Then fold the photocopy along the dotted line of the pattern and cut through both thicknesses of paper, being careful not to cut through the fold.

If the pattern is shown less than full size, find a machine with an enlarging function. We've told you how much to enlarge the pattern to create a project exactly like the one shown. Of course, you can make it any size you choose.

Almost as simple is old reliable tracing paper. Simply trace the pattern and cut it out, following the instructions above for half patterns.

The cut paper ornaments on pages 57–60 have specific directions for transferring patterns.

Herbs &
Flowers

❈ NATURE TREE ❈

Some of the handsomest ornaments are already hanging in the trees outside. Look carefully in your backyard or along the roadside, and consider adding your finds to your own tree. Then fill in the empty spaces with materials from the craft store or from last summer's garden.

Materials

Grapevines or grapevine wreath bases, wasp nests, sumac heads, pinecones, tree lichens, Spanish moss, sprigs of German statice, red eucalyptus, wheat, dried hydrangea blossoms, long cinnamon sticks, brown paper ribbon, craft birds, decorative paper leaves, floral wire

1. If the grapevines are dry and difficult to bend, soak them in warm water overnight. Once they're pliable, spiral them around the tree and allow them to dry.

   If you can't find grapevines, you can buy vine wreath bases. Remove the hardware holding the bases together and soak the vines overnight in warm water. Once the vines are pliable, they'll be happy to uncoil.

2. Wire three or four cinnamon sticks together around the center, leaving long wire tails for attaching the bundle to the tree. Tie a bow of parchment-colored paper ribbon over the wire.

3. To make a tree topper, fashion a large, multi-loop bow of paper ribbon, leaving long streamers. Wire the bow together around the center, leaving long wire ends. Wire stalks of wheat and stems of red eucalyptus to the center of the bow. Tie another knot in the bow to hide the wires and fan out the foliage. Wire the decoration to the top of the tree.

4. Attach the remaining materials to the tree any way you can: with floral wire, hot glue, or just careful positioning.

❈ LUNARIA ORNAMENTS ❈

Pearly lunaria glimmer against a fresh green tree.

Materials

2-1/2-inch-diameter (6 cm) foam ball, about 36 lunaria membranes, tacky glue, glue gun, 3 dried mint leaves, 3 red globe amaranth, floral pin or other push pin, 17-inch (42 cm) length of cord

1. Place a thin film of tacky glue on the back of a lunaria membrane and mold it to the foam ball, holding it firmly until the glue is set.
2. Repeat with each lunaria until the ball is covered, leaving a bare spot about 1/2 inch (1 cm) in diameter at the top.
3. Tie the cord around the floral pin and push the pin into the bare spot; secure it to the ball with a little hot glue. Knot the ends of the cord to form a hanger.
4. Hot-glue the mint leaves in a trefoil shape around the hanger and glue the globe amaranth on top of the leaves.

Ancient Wisdom

Trees figure prominently in a great many religions, often as a source of enlightenment. In Scandinavian legend, the god Odin acquired his wisdom by drinking from the spring at the foot of a mighty ash, so huge that it connected the earth with heaven and hell. In the Old Testament story of the Garden of Eden, Eve was moved to eat the forbidden fruit when she saw that it came from "a tree to be desired to make one wise..."

✖ FLORAL POMANDERS AND WREATHS ✖

Rose-covered pomanders consume multitudes of tiny rosebuds,
but the results are striking. Miniature vine wreaths can be
decorated with a variety of small dried flowers.

Rose Pomanders

Materials

250 tiny rosebuds, foam ball 2-1/2
inches (6 cm) in diameter, glue gun,
7-inch (18 cm) length of ribbon 1/4
inch (6 mm) wide, 10-inch (25 cm)
length of ribbon, floral pin or other
push pin

1. For easier insertion, cut the rosebud stems on the diagonal.
2. Place a dot of hot glue on the
   foam ball and push a rose stem
   into the glue and into the ball.
3. Repeat until the ball is covered
   with roses, leaving a bare spot
   large enough for the floral pin.
4. Form the 7-inch length of ribbon
   into a loop and tie it to the pin.
   Shape the 10-inch ribbon into a
   bow and tie it to the end of the
   pin. Push the pin into the bare
   spot on the ball.

——————— ✖ ———————

Mini Wreath

Materials

Grapevine wreath base 3 inches (8
cm) in diameter, 4-inch (10 cm) piece
of green floral wire, glue gun, 10 to
12 dried cat mint leaves, 4 red
strawflowers, 4 dried rosebuds, 4 tiny
clusters of white annual statice, 5
tiny yellow santolina flowers, 4 sprigs
of lavender

1. Form the wire into a loop and
   attach it to the back of the
   wreath.
2. Hot-glue the dried materials to
   the base, beginning with the
   mint leaves.

❈ LAVENDER POTPOURRI ❈

Plastic potpourri balls have holes in both sides to allow the fragrance to escape.

Materials
3-inch-diameter (7 cm) plastic pot-pourri ball, 1/3 cup (80 ml) lavender flowers, 21-inch (52 cm) length of ribbon, 18-inch (45 cm) length of pearl garland, fine-gauge wire, glue gun, 4 dried mint leaves, 2 pink strawflowers, 2 purple globe amaranth, 2 sprigs pearly everlasting

1. Fill the potpourri ball half full with lavender flowers and close it securely.
2. Form the ribbon into a six-loop bow and wrap its center with wire.
3. Thread the pearl garland through the ball's plastic loop and tie it close to the loop. Position the bow on top of the loop, tie it on with the pearl garland, and knot the ends of the garland to form a hanger.
4. Hot-glue the other materials around the bow in the order listed.

The Origin of the Christmas Tree (Astronomy Version)

One clear December night, Martin Luther was making his way home through the forests of his native Germany. He stopped to admire the stars, which seemed to glitter in the branches of a magnificent evergreen. Entranced by such beauty, Luther went home, cut down a fir tree, set it in his house, and filled the branches with candles.

❧ ROSE-FILLED HEARTS ❧

If your ornaments are pre-
dominantly round, add a
different shape to the tree.

Materials
Hollow, heart-shaped plastic ornament, 1/2 cup (120 ml) dried rose
petals, narrow red metallic ribbon,
glue gun, 2 dried rose leaves, 2
rosebuds, 2 tiny sprigs of white
baby's-breath

1. Open the ornament and fill
   each half with dried rose
   petals. Close the ornament
   securely.
2. Thread a piece of ribbon
   through the clasp to serve as a
   hanger and knot it at the base.
3. Form a six-loop bow and tie it
   over the knot.

4. Hot-glue a rose leaf on each side
   of the heart and a rosebud to
   each leaf. Finish off with tiny
   sprigs of baby's-breath.

The Origin of the Christmas Tree (Forestry Version)

St. Boniface was an eighth-
century English monk sent to
convert the tribes of Germany
to Christianity. One winter solstice, he happened upon a trib-
al chieftain about to sacrifice
his son under a huge oak tree,
to appease the gods and to
bring back the light. Appalled,
St. Boniface seized an axe and
smote the oak one mighty
blow. The oak split down the
middle, revealing a small, perfect fir tree inside. The chieftain (and certainly the son)
were converted on the spot.

❧ FLOWER-FILLED BALL ❧

The clear glass balls available at most Christmas stores are fine
starting points for a crafter.

Materials
Glass ball, dried lavender, globe
amaranth, statice, wired gold ribbon,
glue gun

1. Remove the ornament cap and
   insert the flowers into the ball a
   sprig at a time, creating a pleasing arrangement.
2. Replace the cap, which will help
   hold the flowers in place.
3. Make a bow with long streamers
   and hot-glue it to the neck of the
   ornament.
4. As a finishing touch, hot-glue two
   tiny sprigs of statice and one of
   lavender to the top.

❋ WHITE-AND-SILVER TABLE TREE ❋

Dressed in snowy shades of flowers and foliage, this handsome table tree is resplendent with artemisia, pearly everlasting, yarrow, annual statice, and lamb's-ears. You can make it by hot-gluing any dried white flowers to an artificial green tree.

Materials

Artificial table tree about 2 feet (60 cm) tall with burlap-wrapped base, crocheted place mat or large doily, floral wire, 1-1/2 yards (1.4 m) of wired white ribbon 2 inches (5 cm) wide, large plastic bag, artemisia, pearly everlasting, white annual statice, white yarrow, lamb's-ears

1. Gather the crocheted place mat or doily around the base of the tree and secure it with floral wire or string.
2. Wrap a 24-inch (60 cm) length of ribbon around the base and tie it off. Make a bow from 30 inches (75 cm) of the ribbon and hot-glue it in place. Slip a large plastic bag over the finished base to protect it from glue.
3. Form small bouquets of three or four pieces of artemisia, fanning them out from the stems. Surround the stem ends with hot glue and insert the bouquets between the branches at the bottom of the tree. Working from bottom to top, place artemisia bouquets randomly around the tree, cutting the stems shorter as you move toward the top of the tree.
4. In a similar fashion, make bouquets of pearly everlasting, white yarrow, white annual statice, and lamb's-ears, and hot-glue them randomly around the tree.

Family Tree

All of earth's trees fall into three groups: the broad-leaves, such as oaks and maples; the palms; and the conifers. Ancient plants, conifers have a few defining characteristics. They have hard, narrow leaves known as needles or scales, depending on their shape; they produce cones (hence the term *conifer*) instead of true flowers; and almost all are evergreen.

Conifers grow around the world, most thickly in cold northern climates, where they circle the globe in a ribbon of forest that stretches across North America, Scandinavia, and Siberia. Farther to the south, conifers climb the slopes of cool mountains.

Unlike the broad-leaves, which drop their leaves during a few spectacular weeks in the fall, conifers shed their leaves a few at a time, continually replacing the ones that are lost. With their thick, tough, waxy skin, evergreen needles can survive the cold northern winters. Evergreens have also adapted to the huge snowfalls of the far north. The fir's downward-sloping branches and smooth, flexible leaves shed snow fairly efficiently; much of a heavy, two-foot (60 cm) snow will slide off the branches, rather than breaking them.

❋ HERB BALLS ❋

Herbs are beautiful enough (and fragrant enough) to merit a place on the most gorgeous evergreen. Note: Be sure you really like the penetrating scent of sassafras before you hang it on your tree.

Bay Leaf Ball

Materials

2-1/2-inch-diameter (6 cm) foam ball, about 18 bay leaves, straight pins, tacky glue, glue gun, raffia

1. Select a point on the ball to be the top, and use straight pins to fasten the tips of eight to 10 leaves near that point. With the tacky glue, glue the leaves to the ball one at a time, fanning them out over the ball and holding them firmly in place until they dry.
2. Glue additional leaves to the ball until it is covered.
3. Tie the ball up with raffia, forming the last 12 inches (30 cm) into a loop for hanging.
4. Make a six-loop raffia bow and hot-glue it to the top of the ball.

———— ❋ ————

Lavender Ball

Materials

2-inch-diameter (5 cm) foam ball, about 2/3 cup (160 ml) lavender petals, pie plate or flat dish, brush, tacky glue, raffia, 2 whole lavender blooms, glue gun

1. Place the lavender petals in the pie pan or flat dish.
2. Spread tacky glue onto a section of the foam ball. Press the glued section into the lavender petals and mold them to the ball with your hand.

3. Working section by section, continue in this fashion until the ball is covered.
4. When the glue is dry, tie up the ball with raffia, forming the last 12 inches (30 cm) into a loop for hanging.
5. Hot-glue several lavender blooms to the top of the ball.
6. Form a six-loop raffia bow and hot-glue it over the lavender stems.

———— ❋ ————

Sassafras

Materials

2-inch-diameter (5 cm) foam ball, about 2/3 cup (160 ml) sassafras chips (roots and bark), pie plate or flat dish, brush, tacky glue, raffia, glue gun

1. Place the sassafras chips in the pie plate or flat dish.
2. Spread tacky glue onto a section of the foam ball. Press the glued section into the sassafras chips and mold the chips to the ball with your hand.
3. Repeat with additional sections until the ball is covered with chips.
4. When the glue is dry, tie up the ball with raffia, forming the last 12 inches (30 cm) into a loop for hanging.
5. Make a six-loop raffia bow and hot-glue it to the top of the ball.

———— ❋ ————

Rose Petal Ball

Materials

3-inch-diameter (8 cm) foam ball, 1-1/3 cups (315 ml) dried rose petals, pie plate or flat dish, brush, tacky glue, raffia, glue gun

1. Place the rose petals in the flat dish or pie pan.
2. Spread tacky glue onto a section of the foam ball and press the glued section into the petals. Press the petals into the ball with your hand.
3. Repeat with additional sections until the ball is covered.
4. When the glue is dry, tie up the ball with raffia, forming a loop for hanging from the last 12 inches (30 cm).
5. Make a six-loop raffia bow and hot-glue it to the top of the ball.

The Origin of the Christmas Tree (Life Is Fair Version)

Once upon a time, a poor woodsman was making his way home on a bitter December night. He stumbled upon a small child—lost, hungry, and crying. Despite his own hunger, the woodsman took the child home to his tiny hovel and shared what meager bread he had. The next morning, the woodsman awoke to find a beautiful, shining tree outside his door, hung with all manner of good food and warm clothing. The hungry orphan had been the Christ Child in disguise.

✳ PAINTED POTS ✳

Terra cotta pots with black designs date back at least to ancient Greece. These distinctive ornaments look best when decorated with simple graphic designs—good news for most of us.

Materials

2-inch (5 cm) tall flowerpots; black, fine-tipped permanent marker; small pieces of floral foam (optional); dried flowers or grasses; floral wire

1. Sketch a few designs on paper first, until you find the ones that you like best.

2. Draw your designs on the pots with the permanent marker. If there are bold horizontal lines, make them first. For accuracy, measure down from the lip of the pot and place a few dots on those measurements, then connect the lines. Then fill in the details.

3. Fill the pots with the dried materials of your choice. (A small piece of floral foam in the bottom will make arranging easier.) Ours holds dried red strawflowers.

4. To hang each pot, wrap a piece of green floral wire just under the neck and twist the wire ends around a tree branch.

The Coming of the Christmas Tree (Cleveland Version)

In 1851 the Reverend Henry Schwan set up a Christmas tree in his church in Cleveland, Ohio. Outraged by such a blatant display of paganism, his congregation forced him to remove it. The pastor of another church, moved by his colleague's embarrassment, sent Reverend Schwan's congregation a huge, beautiful evergreen. Unwilling to spurn a Christmas gift (or ministerial solidarity), the congregation allowed the second tree to remain. The church has decorated a Christmas tree every year since then.

❈ SUNFLOWER TABLE TREE ❈

Fill in between the cheerful sunflowers with a variety of natural materials.

Materials

16-inch-tall (40 cm) artificial tree with burlap-wrapped base; glue gun; raffia; faux sunflowers 1-1/2 inches (4 cm) in diameter; green chenille stems; 3- to 4-inch (7 to 10 cm) pieces of straw; tiny cones, berries, or dried flowers; sprays of red berries; decorative pods; 3/16-inch-wide (5 mm) red velvet ribbon; fine-gauge floral wire; dried orange slices; sprigs of dried purple larkspur; sprigs of dried baby's-breath; 2 large, flat lichens

1. Make a raffia bow and hot-glue it to the base of the tree.
2. Wrap single strands of raffia around the tree as garlands, hot-gluing both ends to the branches.
3. Attach the sunflowers to the tree. If yours have plastic stems, remove the stems and hot-glue a short piece of green chenille stem to the back of the flower. Attach the flowers to the tree with the chenille stems.
4. Make the straw bundle ornaments, using the stems of wheat or large wild grasses. Lay six stalks together and wrap the bundle around the center with raffia. Hot-glue tiny cones, berries, and/ or dried flowers to the center. Tie the bundles onto the tree.
5. Hot-glue the sprays of berries and the decorative pods randomly around the tree.
6. Make two-loop bows with the red velvet ribbon and wire them to the tree.
7. Hot-glue the orange slices, larkspur, and baby's-breath randomly around the tree.
8. Hot-glue the lichens to the bottom of the tree.

❈ FLOWER TREE ❈

If you've ever wandered through the dried-flower section of a craft store and wished you could use everything you saw, here's your chance. This flower-loving tree is a natural for sunroom, sewing room, or bedroom.

Materials
Dried and/or silk flowers, floral wire, small gold Christmas balls

1. Make bouquets of the flowers and wire them together around the stems, leaving long wire tails. Vary the size and composition of the bouquets.
2. Wire the bouquets to the tree. In some cases, you'll be able simply to tuck the bouquets among the branches.

NATURE BUNDLES

❋

These collections of
natural evergreens are
striking on a white tree.

Materials
Evergreen sprays, dried weeds
and grasses, dried flowers, sprigs
of berries, tiny cones, metallic
spray paint, floral wire, florist
or parchment paper

1. Wander out into the woods (or
   into your backyard) and collect
   whatever materials catch your
   fancy. Use your imagination and
   be optimistic.
2. Spray-paint whatever looks in
   need of help, using gold and

other metallic paints.
3. Arrange the materials in
   small sprays or bouquets and
   wire them together with
   floral wire. Add some tissue
   paper or parchment paper to
   finish off.

147

❊ HYDRANGEA WALL TREE ❊

If there's no floor or table space left for one more Christmas tree, move to the walls. Artificial wall trees can be dressed up for any room in the house.

Materials

Artificial wall tree about 30 inches (75 cm) tall with one flat side, green chenille stem, glue gun, sprigs of dried artemisia, dried hydrangea flowers, crested celosia flowers

1. To make a non-scratching hanger, form a green chenille craft stem into a loop and attach it to the back of the tree.
2. Straighten the wiry branches of the tree.
3. Hot-glue the artemisia around the sides of the tree.
4. Now hot-glue the hydrangea over the tree, filling it nearly full.
5. Finally, hot-glue crested celosia flowers randomly over the tree.

The Beauty of the Christmas Tree (Military Version)

The story goes like this. During the American Revolution, George Washington decided that Christmas night would be a fine time to attack a division of Hessians—professional German soldiers hired to fight for the British crown—who were encamped outside Trenton, New Jersey. Sure enough. The Hessians, completely engrossed in making merry around a candle-lit Christmas tree, failed to notice the approach of Washington's troops and were defeated.

While serious historians do not leap to confirm this bit of folklore, it is true at least that Hessian troops introduced candle-lit Christmas trees to the children of Newport, Rhode Island.

❋ ROSE TREE ❋

If your den doesn't have enough room for even a table-sized Christmas tree, tuck a tiny one into the bookshelves. If the tree is made of dried roses instead of live evergreens, it will need neither light nor water, and there will still be no mistaking its festive purpose.

Materials

9-inch-tall (22 cm) foam cone, glue gun, 3 cups (700 ml) dried rose petals, 1 dried rosebud about 1 inch (2.4 cm) long, 4 dried rosebuds about 1/2 inch (1.5 cm) long, raffia

1. Holding the foam cone by its tip, cover a small section at the base of the cone with hot glue. Press a handful of dried rose petals into the glued section. Press additional petals into the area until it is covered.
2. Working from bottom to top and section by section, cover the cone with petals. As you near the top, you'll need to hold the cone by the bottom.
3. Hot-glue the large rose to the top of the tree.
4. Wrap raffia around the base of the tree several times, make a six-loop raffia bow, and hot-glue it in place. Hot-glue the small rosebuds to the center of the bow.

Fabric, Yarn, Buttons & Bows

❋ LACE ORNAMENTS ❋

If you long for a Victorian tree, you can create a beauty. Combine purchased ornaments—clip-on candle lights, glass balls and animals, spider webs, a Victorian doll wired to the top of the tree—with simple bows of 1-inch-wide (2.5 cm) lace ribbon. Stiffen the ribbon with fabric softener if necessary, and insert dried flowers into the knots. Add bunches of baby's-breath to fill in around the tree.

Lace Fans

Materials
10-inch (25 cm) length of 6-inch-wide (15 cm) lace ribbon, dried or silk flowers, floral wire, narrow ribbon

1. Pleat the lace end to end accordion style.
2. Wrap a piece of floral wire around the folded fan about 1 inch (2.5 cm) from one end, gathering the lace tightly. Allow the other end to open up, producing a fan shape.
3. Make a bow of the narrow ribbon.
4. Wire the bow to the bottom of the fan, along with a flower or two. Leave wire "tails" behind the fan to wire to the tree branches.

— ❋ —

Puffy Handkerchiefs

Materials
Lace handkerchief, potpourri, dried flowers, floral wire

1. Place a handful of potpourri (or even wadded tissue paper) in the center of the handkerchief and gather the edges up around it.
2. Insert a bouquet of dried flowers into the opening and tie up the bundle with string or floral wire.
3. Allow the edges of the handkerchief to fall down around the ornament to conceal the wire.
4. No need for a hanger; just tuck the ornament on top of a handy branch.

— ❋ —

Lace Doilies

Materials
Crocheted doily, plastic or glass flower, floral wire

1. Insert the flower through the center of the doily.
2. Wire the stem of the flower to the branches.

✻ CHRISTMAS ON THE FARM ✻

If you yearn for Christmas in the country, you'll think you've arrived every time you look at these ornaments—a herd of holsteins, a clothesline full of long johns, some colorful quilts, and even packs left by a couple of hoboes, who stopped at the front gate to cadge a piece of pie. Only the quilts require sewing.

Long John Garland

Materials
(for 6 feet [1.8 m] of garland)
2 yards of ribbon 1/4 inch (6 mm) wide; 9- by 12-inch (22 X 30 cm) square of red felt; fabric glue; gold sequins

1. Cut nine long johns and nine seat flaps from the red felt.
2. Glue the flaps in the appropriate places. Glue sequins at the top corners, to resemble buttons. Allow to dry.
3. Glue one long john every 8 inches (20 cm) along the ribbon, attaching the underwear at about shoulder height.

Cow

Materials
9- x 12-inch (22 X 30 cm) squares of felt in white and black; squares of felt in brown and gold (optional); fabric glue; fabric stiffener; 8-inch (20 cm) length of narrow ribbon; 1/4-inch-diameter (6 mm) bell

1. Make one pattern for the cow, one pattern for the cow's black markings, and, if you plan to fence your herd, two fence patterns.
2. Cut the entire cow out of white felt; cut one piece of black felt in the shape of the cow's markings. If desired, cut one brown fence and one gold fence.
3. Glue the black pieces onto the white with the fabric glue. Allow to dry. Glue the gold fence onto the brown one, allowing some of the brown to show.
4. Stiffen each cow and fence with the fabric stiffener, following the manufacturer's instructions. Allow to dry.
5. String the bell on a 4-inch (10 cm) length of ribbon and tie around the cow's neck, adding a spiffy bow. Secure with a dab of glue.
6. If desired, glue the cow to the fence.
7. To make a hanger, glue a 4-inch loop of ribbon to the top center of the ornament.

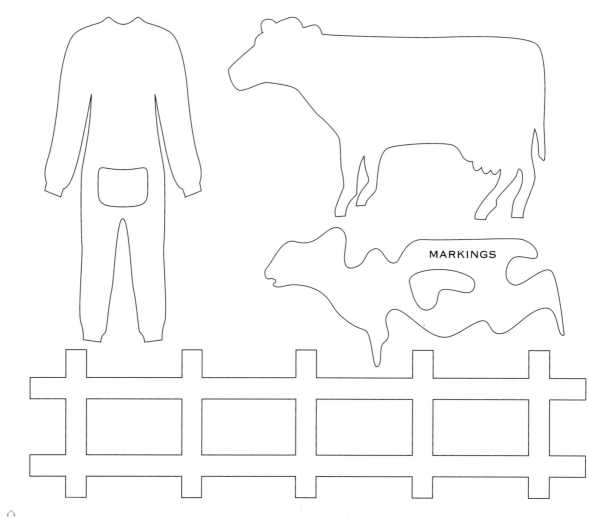

MARKINGS

Quilt

Materials (for 6 quilts)
About 1/4 yard (22 cm) of patchwork print fabric, 1/4 yard of complementary print or solid fabric, thin batting, 1 yard (90 cm) of ribbon 1/8 inch (3 mm) wide, sewing machine, large-eyed needle

1. For each quilt, cut out a rectangle of the quilt print and the complementary fabric, adding 1/4 inch (6 mm) seam allowances. The size of the ornaments will depend on the patchwork print; make them small enough to hang on the tree but large enough to include complete squares in the pattern.
2. With right sides together, sew a patchwork piece and a complementary piece together around the edges, leaving a 2-inch (5 cm) opening for turning.
3. Turn the quilts right side out and stuff with batting or a thin layer of fiberfill.
4. Stitch along all edges and along all pattern lines, creating a quilted look.
5. Thread the needle with a 4-inch (10 cm) piece of ribbon, pull the ribbon through a corner of the ornament, and knot the ends of the ribbon to form a hanger.

Hobo Stick

Materials
6-inch (15 cm) length of dowel 1/8 or 1/4 inch (3 or 6 mm) in diameter, 6-inch square of fabric, 4-inch (10 cm) length of narrow ribbon, fabric glue, fiberfill or wadded paper

1. Form the ribbon into a loop and glue it 1-1/2 inches (4 cm) from one end of the dowel.
2. Place the fiberfill or wadded paper in the center of the fabric square.
3. Fold two opposite corners over the center, tucking one corner under the other. Fold the other two corners over the first two and tie them in a half knot.
4. Place a dot of glue on the knot. Place the dowel on the knot, so that the loop of ribbon sits, facing up, over the knot.
5. Tie the fabric ends over the dowel in a square knot. Secure with a final dot of glue.

And a Tip of the Stocking Cap, Too

Wilderness lovers, take heart: Virtually all of the 40 million Christmas trees Americans buy each year come from commercial tree farms, not from natural forests.

While a tree farm isn't as ecologically valuable as uncut wilderness, it's nothing to sneeze at, either. In this age of air pollution and acid rain, an industry that plants, re-plants, and cares for thousands of oxygen-producing, carbon-monoxide-consuming trees every year deserves a bit of environmental respect.

Cathedral Windows is a traditional quilt pattern, but you don't have to know how to quilt in order to make these stunning ornaments. Since the inset "windows" are only 1-1/2 inches (6 cm) square, you can use leftover scraps of various fabrics.

Materials

2 7-inch (17.5 cm) squares of gold lamé fabric, 2 1-1/2-inch (6 cm) squares of red-and-green fabric, matching thread, sewing machine, fiberfill, needle, gold cord

1. Fold a 7-inch square in half and stitch up the ends with a 1/4-inch (6 mm) seam. See Figure 1.

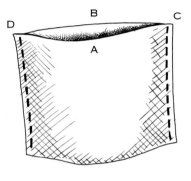

FIGURE 1

2. Pull outward at points A and B, so that C and D come together. Sew a 1/4-inch seam across the top, leaving a 2- or 3-inch (5 to 8 cm) opening in the center for turning. See Figure 2.

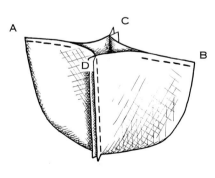

FIGURE 2

3. Turn the square right side out through the opening. Pull the corners out and press the square flat. Blindstitch the opening closed. See Figure 3.

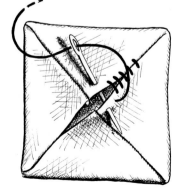

FIGURE 3

4. Fold the four corners so they meet in the center and press closed. The press marks will supply the seamlines. See Figure 4.

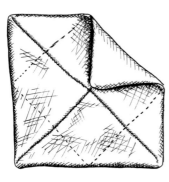

FIGURE 4

5. Place two folded squares back to back. Sew them together along two opposite creases. See Figure 5.

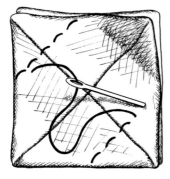

FIGURE 5

6. Fold the four corner flaps of each square toward the center and tack them together where they meet. See Figure 6.

FIGURE 6

7. Pull the two joined squares open, so that the seamline is in the center and the tacked flaps meet at each edge. You should see a diamond within a square. See Figure 7.

FIGURE 7

8. Center a small red-and-green fabric inset inside the diamond.
9. Fold the center of the loose edges of gold fabric down over the inset, creating a curved effect. See Figure 8. Whipstitch in place.

FIGURE 8

10. In the same fashion, sew a fabric inset to the other side of the ornament.
11. Whipstitch one open edge of the ornament closed. Stuff with fiberfill. Whipstitch the remaining edge closed.
12. Thread a needle with the gold cord. Bring the cord through one corner of the ornament and knot it, creating a loop for hanging.

Is It Fresh?

How can you spot a freshly cut tree, one that will look good and hold its needles through the holiday season?

Bend a single needle gently between your thumb and forefinger. If the needle is flexible, the tree is fresh. If the needle is brittle and breaks in two, the tree is aging rapidly. Run your hand down the branches. For most species, the needles should feel soft and flexible, not dry and stiff.

Lift the tree a few inches off the ground by its trunk and drop it back down. (If you're not up to hoisting a full-sized evergreen, shake a few branches briskly back and forth.) If needles shower onto the ground, the tree is advanced in years.

Finally, look for a tree that's locally grown; it may well be fresher than one that's been trucked across the country.

✳ WILD, WILD WEST ✳

If anyone in your household is still at the cowboy stage of development, you might wanna mosey on over to the old fabric drawer and make a tree that'll tickle their fantasies.

You can either photocopy the patterns at 200% or use them as guides to draw your own at any size you like.

Sheriff's Star

Materials (for 12 stars)
Poster board, 1/2 yard (45 cm) metallic fabric, glue stick, sewing machine with black thread, metallic braid to match fabric, matching sequins

1. Following the pattern, cut 12 stars from the poster board.
2. Cut pieces of fabric slightly larger than the stars. Apply the glue stick to the poster board and press a piece of fabric onto the star. Glue a second piece of fabric to the other side. Allow to dry.
3. Trim the fabric loosely around the stars.
4. Following the edge of the star, stitch through all layers about 1/8 inch (1.5 mm) from the edge of the poster board. Trim the fabric even with the paper.
5. Make a loop from the braid and glue it to one tip of the star. Glue a sequin over the glued end.

Cowboy Boots

Materials (for 6 boots)
9- by 12-inch (23 X 30 cm) piece of felt, decorative cord, snowflake sequin, fiberfill, sewing machine, fabric glue

1. Cut two pieces for each boot.
2. Wrong sides together, stitch around the boot close to the edge, leaving an opening for stuffing. Make a loop from a 1-1/2-inch (4 cm) piece of cord and stitch it into the seam at the top rear of the boot.
3. Stuff the boot to a medium fluff with fiberfill and machine stitch the opening closed.
4. Using the photo as a guide, glue braid to the boot. Glue the snowflake sequin to the heel as a spur.

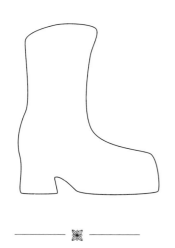

Bandanna Ornament

Materials (for 1 bandanna)
6-inch (15 cm) square of bandanna print material, fabric stiffener, narrow ribbon, fabric glue

1. Saturate the fabric with the stiffener, following the manufacturer's instructions.
2. Flatten the square. Then bring two opposite corners together to form a triangle.
3. Tie the corners into a loose knot and shape the projects with your fingers to look like a neckerchief. Allow to dry.
4. Make a loop of ribbon and glue it to the top fold of the bandanna.

Hobby Horse

Materials
Craft felt in two colors, fabric glue, 4-inch (10 cm) length of fringe, 14 inches (35 cm) of narrow ribbon, 4 sequins, fiberfill

1. Cut two horse heads from felt; cut two ears from a contrasting felt.
2. Glue the fringe around the top and back of one head piece, using the photo (or a horse) as a guide. Trim off the excess on the bottom.
3. Make a loop from a 3-inch ((4 cm) piece of ribbon and glue it to the crown of the head piece, on top of the fringe.
4. Glue the second head piece to the first, working near the edges and leaving the bottom open.
5. Glue the ears to opposite sides of the head.
6. Glue ribbon around the nose, beginning and ending at the position for the sequin (see the photo). Trim the end.
7. To make the harness, glue ribbon onto the head, beginning at the same spot as for the nose. Leave a loop of about 4 inches for a bridle.
8. Glue a sequin at the intersection of the nose ribbon and the harness.

9. Glue sequins in place for eyes.
10. Stuff head lightly and push the dowel into the stuffing. Glue the bottom edges together.

Cowboy Hats

Materials (for 2 hats)
5-inch (13 cm) circle of felt, fabric stiffener, fabric glue, shot glass or similar cylinder, 1 yard (90 cm) decorative braid or narrow ribbon

1. Cut the felt circle in half.
2. Bring the two corners of a semi-circle together and, either by machine or by hand, sew the straight edges together from the corner to within 3/4 inch (2 cm) of the point. You should have a cone shape. Repeat with the other semicircle.

I Want That One, Daddy

The first known Christmas tree market appeared in 1531 on a street corner in the Alsatian town of Strasbourg. Every year since then, Christmas trees have been sold on that same corner. In the early days, townspeople were forbidden by law to have more than one tree, and it could be no more than "eight shoe lengths" tall.

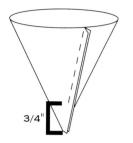

3/4"

3. Saturate one cone with fabric stiffener, following the manufacturer's instructions. Squeeze out the excess; the cone should be wet but not drippy.

4. Place the shot glass upside down on a piece of waxed paper and place the fabric cone over the bottom of the glass. Using the glass as a guide, shape the felt into a hat, using the photo (or a cowboy) as a guide. Turn up the bottom edges to make the brim, compress the hatband area, pull up on the crown, and crimp the top. There will be a hole in the "ditch" that runs along the crown. Continue to handle it as it dries to encourage it to retain its shape. When it seems stable, remove it from the glass and shape the second hat. If you're not pleased with a hat as it stiffens, saturate it again with fabric stiffener and start over.

5. When the hat is completely dry, glue the cord or ribbon around the crown, leaving two 2-inch (5 cm) ends to tie to one side. When the glue is dry, tie the two ends in a square knot and trim the ends.

6. To make a hanger, form an 8-inch ((20 cm) length of braid into a loop. Using a crochet hook or something similar, pull the loop through the hole in the hat, working from bottom to top. Tie the ends together into a knot under the hat and pull the knot up into the hat.

Holsters

Materials
9- by 12-inch (23 X 30 cm) square of felt, sewing machine, fabric glue, 3 large star sequins, small candy cane

1. Cut one of each pattern piece from the felt. Also cut a piece of felt 1/2 inch by 6 inches (1.25 X 15 cm).

2. Using a decorative "blanket" stitch or a wide zigzag, stitch across the top of the front (smaller) piece.

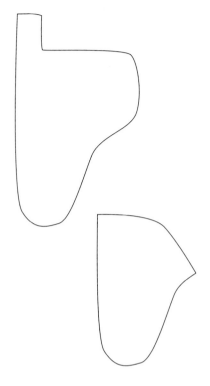

3. Place the small piece on top of the large one. Stitch around the edge of the two pieces.

4. Glue the sequins to the holster, using the photo as a guide.

5. Form the long piece of felt into a loop, overlapping the ends by 2 inches (5 cm). Stitch across the belt near the inside end. Glue sequins down the belt.

6. Glue the holster to the belt.

7. Glue a loop of braid to the back of the holster and place a candy cane in the pocket.

No, I Said That One, Daddy

In 1851 a farmer from the Catskill Mountains of upstate New York started the first known Christmas tree business in the United States. Mike Carr shipped fir trees by steamboat to New York City in early December and proceeded to sell them in Washington Market, near Greenwich Street.

A mere 30 years later, more than 600 tree sellers were competing for customers in Washington Market. A small tree sold for 10 cents, a large one for a quarter.

The angels and fabric chains on this homey tree require no sewing. In fact, you can turn your best linen handkerchief into a Christmas angel, then untie it, unharmed, after the holidays are over. Small, unhemmed scraps of muslin also make delightfully down-home heavenly hosts. Small bunches of white baby's-breath tied up with raffia serve as fillers.

Angel With Raffia Wings

Materials

10- to 12-inch-square (25 to 30 cm) handkerchief, ball of polyester fiberfill about 2 inches (5 cm) in diameter, heavy thread, raffia, 8-inch (20 cm) piece of medium-gauge floral wire

1. To make the head, fold one edge of the handkerchief 2-1/2 inches (6 cm) to one side. Place the fiberfill ball between the layers of fabric at the center. Tie thread tightly under the fiberfill (see Figure 1) in a secure knot. Trim the thread ends.

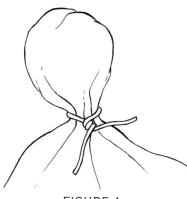

FIGURE 1

2. To make the arms, tie a top corner of the fabric into a knot close to the head (see Figure 2). Repeat for the opposite corner for the other arm.

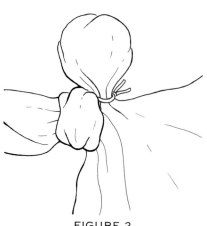

FIGURE 2

3. For the halo, wrap the floral wire with raffia. Bend it so that you have a loop in the center about 1-1/2 inches (4 cm) in diameter and a vertical "stand" in the back. Tie the halo to the angel's neck with the heavy thread.
4. Make a raffia bow to serve as wings, leaving long, graceful streamers, and tie the wings to the neck with heavy thread.
5. Tie a piece of jute around the neck, finishing with a two-loop bow.

--- ✳ ---

Angel With Paper Wings

1. Make the angel by following Steps 1 through 3 above.
2. Cut a piece of beige paper ribbon about 5 inches (13 cm) long. If necessary, trim the ends to make smaller wings for smaller angels. Gather the ribbon in the center and tie it up with heavy thread. Tie the wings to the angel's neck.

--- ✳ ---

Strung Hearts

Materials

5-inch (12 cm) squares of fabric (2 for each heart), matching thread, sewing machine, 18 inches (45 cm) of jute cord or other rustic-looking cord, large needle, fiberfill

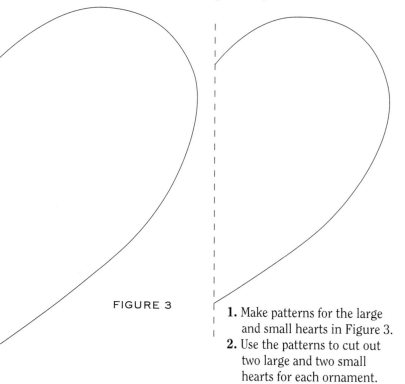

FIGURE 3

1. Make patterns for the large and small hearts in Figure 3.
2. Use the patterns to cut out two large and two small hearts for each ornament.

3. For each heart, place two same-sized pieces right sides together and sew around the pieces 1/4 inch (6 mm) from the edge, leaving a 1-inch (2.5 cm) opening.
4. Turn the heart right side out through the opening and stuff the heart with fiberfill. Sew the opening closed by hand.
5. Thread the large needle with the jute cord. Take the needle vertically through the center of each heart, knotting the jute just below each heart (see Figure 4) and tying a two-loop bow just above. Form the excess jute into a loop for hanging.

Fabric Chains

Materials
Bright printed fabrics, iron-on interfacing, fabric glue

1. Iron the interfacing to the wrong side of the fabric, following the manufacturer's instructions.
2. Cut the interfaced fabrics into strips about 3/4 inch (2 cm) wide and 6 inches (15 cm) long. Form them into chains (make sure the interfacing is on the inside), overlapping the ends and gluing them closed.

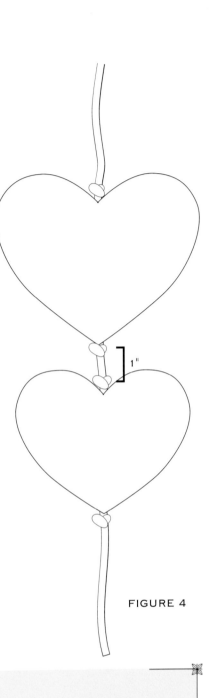

FIGURE 4

Care and Feeding

To extend the life of your *cut tree*, saw off the bottom inch (2.5 cm) of the trunk immediately, and stand the tree in a bucket of water away from wind, sun, and heat, until you're ready to decorate it. Fresh trees will drink a gallon of water a day, so invest in a tree stand with a large reservoir and check the water level daily.

If you're considering a dug-up *live tree* that you can re-plant after the holidays, keep in mind that they're extremely heavy; make sure someone in the household can lug one around. When shopping, look for a rootball that's large, intact, moist, and wrapped in burlap. Keep the tree in a cool place until it's time to decorate it. Once Christmas is over, plant it immediately if the ground isn't frozen hard. If it is, store the tree in a sheltered place with the rootball packed in straw until the next thaw. Spruces are the best candidates for live trees. They're the toughest of the common Christmas varieties and most likely to survive.

✄ God's Eye ✄

An ancient design, a simple God's-eye makes a good ornament whether done in fine or heavy yarn. The one shown uses variegated yarn. You can also change colors at any point in the construction by tying a different color yarn to the old color at the back of the ornament. A God's-eye can be made larger or smaller, depending on your preference.

Materials
2 popsicle-type craft sticks or 2 pieces of similar wood, glue, yarn

1. Cross the two pieces of wood in the center and glue them together. Allow to dry.
2. Hold the yarn behind the crossed wood so that the "tail" is in the lower left quadrant.
3. Bring the yarn to the front through the lower right quadrant and loop it over the right arm (see Figure 1).

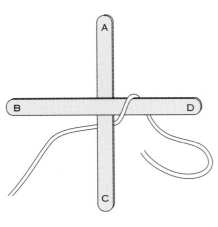

FIGURE 1

4. Bring the yarn around the right arm, then take it diagonally to the upper left quadrant (see Figure 2).

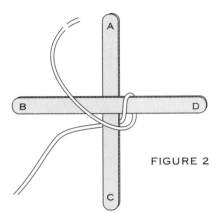

FIGURE 2

5. Turn the cross a quarter turn to the right.
6. Bring the yarn down behind and around the right arm, then diagonally to the upper left quadrant (see Figure 3).

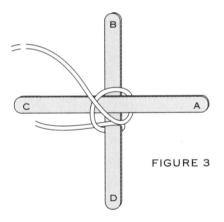

FIGURE 3

7. Turn the cross a quarter turn.
8. Continue this sequence ad infinitum. The movement is always down behind and around the right arm, diagonally up to the left, quarter turn of the cross. Each time you go around, try to lay the yarn right next to the yarn that's already there.
9. For several passes your yarn will form a giant X. Eventually, a diamond will appear in the center of the X.
10. When the God's-eye is the size you want (or when you're about to run out of sticks), glue the end to the back of the ornament.
11. Many people finish at this point, leaving the wooden ends extending from the yarn. If desired, you can add tassels to the ends. Just form a bundle of yarn 4 inches (10 cm) long, fold it in the center, and tie it around the "neck." Tie the tassel to one of the arms, shaggy end out. Make three more tassels for the remaining arms.

❈ TEDDY BEAR TREE ❈

If your daughter has a well-loved collection of bears, gather them together for a tree she will remember when childhood is long past. Some bears can be tucked into the branches; others will need to be wired respectfully to the tree. Fill in around the bears with lace fans (see fan-making instructions on page 27) and burgundy satin balls. And if the congregation isn't quite large enough, add some new members.

Materials
5- by 10-inch (13 X 25 cm) scrap of fabric, fiberfill, sewing machine, narrow ribbon, tapestry needle. For optional tutu: 2- by 72-inch (5 X 180 cm) piece of netting, fabric glue, extra ribbon

1. Cut two bears from the fabric.
2. Right sides together, sew the bears together, leaving a 1-inch (2.5 cm) opening for turning.
3. Turn the piece right side out and stuff with fiberfill. Stitch the opening closed.
4. If the bear wants a tutu, fold the strip of netting into about five layers and baste one long edge together. Gather the basted edge to match the bear's waist and tie off the gathering stitches. Straight stitch over the gathers several times for stability and trim the gathered edge evenly, within 1/8 inch (3 mm) of the stitching. Fit the skirt around the bear and tie it on securely. Add touches of fabric glue for security. Tie on a ribbon sash.
5. Thread ribbon through the tapestry needle and draw the ribbon through the back of the head and tie a 1-inch loop for hanging. Tie a piece of ribbon around the neck.

Safe Season

Go ahead and check your Christmas lights for shorts or frayed wires before you put them on the tree. (You have to replace all those dead bulbs anyhow.) And as delightful as it is to come home to a lit Christmas tree, it's the better part of valor to turn the lights off when the tree is home alone.

Finally, Dickensian fantasies notwithstanding, no completely sane person would attach candles to a Christmas tree *and then light them.* Consider 50 small fires on a tree that becomes better kindling with every day that passes—all inside your house. Christmas tree lights are available that look exactly (and safely) like miniature candles.

❈ TEMARI BALLS ❈

An ancient Japanese craft, temari balls are foam balls wrapped with thread—lots of thread. The designs are made with embroidery floss. The balls make stunning tree ornaments and are not difficult to do, but they require lots of patience.

Materials

Foam ball, serrated knife, jingle bell (optional), transparent tape, facial tissues, 250-yard (230 m) spool of sewing thread (for a foam ball that's 2-1/2-inches, or 6 cm, in diameter), paper, 4 skeins of 6-strand embroidery floss in various colors (or equivalent yardage of 5/2 perle cotton), metallic thread, serrated knife, measuring tape, tapestry needle size 18 to 24

Preparing the Ball

1. If you'd like a bell inside the ornament, cut the foam ball in half with the serrated knife and scoop out a cavity in each half that's about 3/4 inch (2 cm) deep. Place the bell in one of the cavities and tape the ball back together. If you don't want your ornament to jingle, skip this step.

2. Separate a facial tissue into two thin layers. Wrap one of the layers around the ball, to provide a soft base for wrapping and stitching. (For a larger ball, wrap two layers.)

3. Start to wrap the ball with the sewing thread, holding the tissue and the beginning of the thread in place with the first few loops. Continue to wind the thread around the ball in a random pattern until the ball is completely covered. When the ball is covered, thread a needle onto the end of the thread and secure the "tail" by passing the needle under several of the wrapping threads.

Post-Christmas Blues

Evergreen needles are slower to decompose than the leaves of broad-leaved trees, and they decay into a very acid humus. The acid leaf litter and the year-round shade in a thick coniferous forest make an inhospitable nursery for most seedlings. Light-filled openings between evergreen trees are usually occupied by acid-loving plants, such as ferns and toadstools.

God's-Eye Design

(See the three blue balls in the photo on page 45.)

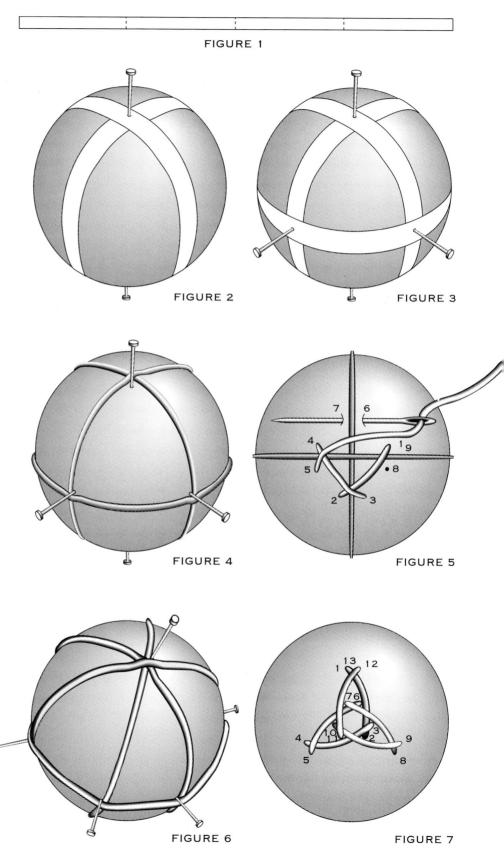

FIGURE 1

1. Cut three strips of paper about 1/4 inch (6 mm) wide and exactly as long as the circumference of the ball. Fold the strips in half lengthwise, then in quarters. Unfold the papers and mark a line at each fold mark (see Figure 1).

2. Cross two paper strips at their centers, so that the center marks intersect, and pin the crossed strips to the ball with a straight pin. This will be the "North Pole" of your ball. Bring the two strips around the center of the ball and pin them at the "South Pole" (see Figure 2). If you need to use extra pins temporarily to hold the strips in place, feel free. Just make sure there's one pin at the North Pole and one at the South Pole.

3. Circle the third strip of paper around the ball at the "Equator," matching the various marks to be sure it's centered between the two poles. The strips should divide the ball into eight segments: four above the equator and four below (see Figure 3).

4. If you used extra pins to hold the paper strips in place, remove all but the ones at the intersections. Tear the paper strips away.

5. Thread the needle with perle cotton in a color that contrasts with the wrapping thread. This will be your guide string.

6. Secure the guide string at the north pole by slipping the needle under a few wrapping threads, then looping the string around the North Pole pin. Take the thread around the ball, securing it at the South Pole and again at the North Pole. Carry the thread around the ball again, dividing the ball into four segments. Secure and cut the thread. Carry a new guide thread around the

FIGURE 2

FIGURE 3

FIGURE 4

FIGURE 5

FIGURE 6

FIGURE 7

Equator, securing it at the pins. You now have eight segments (see Figure 4).

7. Thread the needle with the embroidery floss. Secure the floss by taking the needle under the wrapping threads about 1 inch (2.5 cm), exiting to the right of a guide string very close to the North Pole pin—Point 1 in Figure 5. Follow the diagram in Figure 5, turning the ball counterclockwise. Bring the thread over the next guide string (Point 2), then back under it and a few wrapping threads (Point 3), then over the next guide string (Point 4), then back under it and a few wrapping threads (Point 5), and so on, moving from guide string to guide string. Keep going around the ball counterclockwise. After a few rows, the threads will begin to form a

square. Change colors of floss as you desire. Stop when you have reached halfway to the Equator.

8. Make additional God's-eyes at each intersection of the guide strings.

9. To make a hanger, loop a piece of floss or metallic thread through a handy guide string.

Six-Pointed Design
(See the pink ball in the photo.)

1. As for the God's-eye, use paper strips and straight pins to divide the ball into segments. This time, however, use three strips of paper to divide the ball into six vertical segments between the North and South poles. Add another strip for the Equator, and you have 12 segments—six above the Equator and six below.

2. Using embroidery floss, make a God's-eye at the North Pole, fol-

lowing the previous instructions. Because of the additional guide strings, this God's-eye will have six sides instead of four. On the pink ball in the photo, the God's-eye is done in blue floss.

3. Work the three-pointed design by following the diagram in Figure 7. Again, you are securing the thread each time by going under the guide string and a few wrapping threads, then looping the floss back around the guide string.

4. Change colors of floss as desired. The three-pointed design will build from the inside lines to the outside lines. On the pink ball, for example, the first threads were the purple ones adjacent to the blue God's-eye. The second set were yellow, the third green, and so on.

⚜ BUTTONS AND BOWS ⚜

⚜ BUTTONS AND BOWS ⚜

If your button box is overflowing with interesting specimens that have outlived the garments they once held together, combine your favorites with colorful ribbons and think of them as tree ornaments. A paper chain makes a good filler (see page 57 for instructions on making paper garlands).

Materials
Red, white, and gold ribbons; fine-gauge floral wire; buttons; glue gun, or needle plus very heavy thread

1. Form a two- to six-loop bow with the ribbon, leaving streamers about the length of the loops. Wire it around the center, leaving long wire ends for attaching to the tree.
2. If you don't want to use the button again, simply hot-glue it to the center of the bow, using as little glue as possible. If you want to salvage the button after Christmas, thread a 5-inch (13 cm) piece of thread onto the needle and, starting at the back, loop the thread through two of the button's holes. Remove the needle and tie the thread ends around the center of the bow.

   Note: For security, use the heaviest thread (or the thinnest cord) that will go through the button holes.

⚜ BUTTON BALLS ⚜

A bowl of old buttons at a flea market provided the inspiration and the raw materials for these ornaments.

Materials
Buttons, white satin balls, glue gun, glitter glue sticks, narrow ribbon

1. Apply hot glitter glue to a section of the ball and press in the buttons; the glue will be visible between the buttons, so choose a color that complements the buttons.
2. For the two-layered look on the balls at left and top, add a second layer of buttons, positioning them in the spaces left by the first layer and securing them with dollops of glitter glue.
3. Tie a piece of narrow ribbon in a loop for a hanger.

Paper

❈ PAPIER-MACHE ORNAMENTS ❈

Now that craft stores carry commercially prepared papier-mâché in jars, the formerly time-consuming medium is accessible to just about anybody. These handsome ornaments are just rolled, cut, and painted with acrylic paints. Be sure always to let each color of paint dry before you add details in another color on top of the first.

Making the Ornaments

Materials

Commercial papier-mâché, plastic wrap, rolling pin, pliable wire, wire cutters, plastic knives and/or plastic modeling tools, baking sheet, aluminum foil, acrylic gesso, acrylic paints, paintbrushes with medium and fine tips, acrylic sealer spray

1. Make the papier-mâché according to the package instructions.
2. Lay a sheet of plastic wrap on a level work surface. Place a piece of papier-mâché the size of a tennis ball on the plastic wrap. (That much papier-mâché will make six to eight ornaments). Cover it with another sheet of plastic wrap, and use a rolling pin to roll the pulp out to a thickness of about 1/4 inch (6 mm). Peel off the top layer of plastic wrap. Using a plastic knife or modeling tool, cut the desired shapes. With moistened fingers carefully lift the shapes onto a foil-covered baking sheet.
3. Cut the wire into 2-inch (5 cm) pieces, one for each ornament. Form a loop at the center of the wire by twisting the wire ends together (see Figure 1), and imbed the ends (not the loop itself) in the ornament. With damp fingers, smooth the pulp back into place and smooth any lumpy edges.
4. Let the ornaments air-dry for two days, turning them several times so that both sides dry evenly and the edges don't curl. If you're in a hurry, put the baking sheet into a 200°F (93°C) oven for 45 minutes.

FIGURE 1

Drying times may vary with the thickness of the ornaments, so check them frequently.

5. When the ornaments are dry, apply a coat of acrylic gesso (available in art supply stores and some craft shops), to give you a smooth, paintable surface that won't soak up enormous amounts of paint. Allow the gesso to dry.
6. Paint the ornaments and allow to dry.
7. When all paint has dried, spray the ornaments with acrylic sealer.

Parrots

These ornaments were decorated with metallic paint pens, which are easier to control than paints and paintbrushes. Acrylic paints, however, would work fine. Since real parrots wear plumage in colors that would put a Disney animator to shame, feel free to select any brilliant color you like for these birds. Your ornament will look more like a parrot if you sketch in the beak and eyes and define the neck by changing color.

Fruit Slices (page 52)

Apple: Paint one side of the slice and the edges bright red. Allow to dry. Paint the other side—the flesh—with white into which you've mixed a tiny bit of yellow. Add details of the stem, core, and seeds in brown.

Pear: The flesh is white with a bit more yellow than the apple. Add details of stem, core, and seeds with brown. Paint the other side and the edges of the ornament with bright green lightened with a little yellow.

Orange: Paint one side white. Carefully paint orange sections onto the white base, leaving a white rind, a small white circle in the center, and white lines between each section. Paint white lines radiating from the center in a random fashion and white seeds close to the center in some sections. Outline each seed in brown. Brush diluted yellow over the entire surface. Paint the edges and the other side of the ornament orange. Add dots of white and then brush with diluted yellow.

Lemon: Paint one side of the ornament white. Carefully add the yellow flesh, leaving a white rind and a white line down the center. Add white seeds close to the center line, then outline them in brown. Paint white lines radiating from the center line in a random fashion. Paint the edges and the other side yellow, then add dots of white.

Banana: Paint one side yellow mixed with white. Add a brown line along the center and small dots near this line for seeds.

Fruit Bowl

Make the ornaments as described in Preparing the Ornaments, with an additional touch. For the strawberry and the bunch of grapes, shape small bits of papier-mâché into leaves and add them to the fruit when you make the ornaments. (Leaves can be added at any point—whether the fruit is wet or dry—but you'll have to wait for them to dry as well.)

Strawberry: Paint the berry red and its leaves dark green. Lightly brush pale green over the dark green on the leaves. Add bright yellow dots for the seeds.

Banana: Paint it bright yellow. Add brown lines and dots.

Grapes: Paint the fruit dark purple and the leaves dark green. Brush light green over the leaves. Use light purple and white to paint the individual grapes. Each grape needs a semi-circular white highlight to look round.

Watermelon: Paint one side and the edges of the ornament light green. When that is dry, add stripes of dark green. Paint the flesh bright red, leaving a uniform border of white rind. Add black dots for seeds.

❈ HANDMADE PAPER ❈

Handmade paper is a beautiful substance, with an interesting texture and fascinating flecks of whatever raw materials went into it. Small scraps of it can be used to make arresting tree ornaments.

Materials
6- by 9-inch (15 by 23 cm) sheet of handmade paper or other thick, soft paper, foam ball 2 to 4 inches (5 to 10 cm) in diameter, white glue, brush, raffia

1. Tear the paper into irregular pieces about 1 or 2 inches square (2.5 or 5 cm).
2. Soak the pieces in a mixture of one-half glue and one-half water until damp.
3. Brush the surface of the ball with undiluted glue and press the damp pieces of paper onto the surface. The pieces should overlap; make sure there are no gaps.
4. Set the balls aside in a warm place to dry.
5. Tie the ball with raffia, dividing the ball into four vertical segments. Knot the ends to form a loop.

❈ PAPER WITH GOLD WIRE AND BEADS ❈

Gold-toned wire and off-white beads add festive touches
to handmade paper.

Materials

6- by 9-inch (15 by 23 cm) sheet of
handmade paper or other thick, soft
paper, foam ball 2 to 4 inches (5 to 10
cm) in diameter, white glue, brush,
20- to 28-gauge wire in gold or silver
color, needle the same diameter as
the wire, beads, straight pins

1. Tear the paper into irregular
   pieces about 1 or 2 inches
   square (2.5 or 5 cm).

2. Soak the pieces in a mixture of
   one-half glue and one-half water
   until damp.

3. Brush the surface of the ball with
   undiluted glue and press the
   damp pieces of paper onto the
   surface. The pieces should overlap; make sure there are no gaps.

4. Pierce the top of the ball with the
   needle. Insert the wire into and
   through the ball. Secure the wire
   end at the bottom of the ball by

threading it through a bead,
bending the wire back up over
the bead, and twisting it around
itself.

5. Wrap the other end of the wire
   around the ball in an irregular
   pattern, adding various beads as
   you go. Attach the wire to the
   ball as needed by inserting a
   straight pin into the ball and
   twisting the wire around it.

6. Set aside to dry in a warm place.

✳ CUT PAPER ORNAMENTS ✳

Ordinary paper becomes extraordinary when it's cut into festive shapes and hung on a Christmas tree. Ornaments can be cut from colored paper instead of white, if you prefer.

Materials
Medium-weight paper, sharp-pointed scissors, craft knife, string or decorative cord, artist's tape (or other easily removable tape), push pin

1. Copy the design from the book onto scratch paper and cut out the pattern. Cut out both the overall shape and all the interior spaces.
2. Fold in half the paper to be used for the ornament.
3. Place the pattern on the folded paper, positioning the dotted line on the fold.
4. Trace the pattern onto the paper. Be sure to include all interior openings.
5. Cut out the ornament, using the scissors for the outside and the craft knife for the interior spaces. *Do not cut through the fold.*
6. Repeat Steps 2 through 5, so that you have two identical cutout pieces of paper.
7. Place one cutout on top of the other, aligning them precisely. Tape the edges together with artist's tape.
8. If you want to decorate the ornament with pinpricks, do so now, punching a push pin through both layers of paper at regular intervals around the ornament. (The star and the heart shown in the photos are decorated with pinpricks.)
9. Lay a ruler along the center line and pencil light dots at 1/4-inch (6 mm) intervals. Make a small hole at each mark with a push pin.
10. Thread a needle with thread the same color as the paper. Don't

knot the thread but do leave a 6-inch (15 cm) tail. Starting at the top, use the holes to sew the two pieces together with a running stitch (over, under, over, under). When you've taken the thread through the bottom hole, turn the ornament over and sew back up to the top. There will be thread between every two holes on both sides of the ornament.
11. Make a loop for hanging by knotting the thread ends at the top of the ornament.
12. Remove the tape and bend the four segments at right angles to each other.

--- ✳ ---

Garlands

Materials
Same as above

1. Copy the design from the book onto scratch paper and cut out the pattern. Cut out both the overall shape and all the interior spaces.
2. Accordion-fold a piece of paper. The number of layers of paper you end up with will be the number of angels or stars in your garland. Make sure the folded paper is as wide as you want the images to be.
3. Trace the pattern onto the folded paper.
4. Cut out the figure, being careful not to cut through the dotted lines on either side of the figure.
5. Unfold the garland and hang it on your tree.

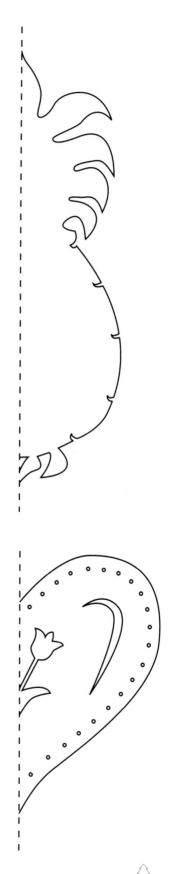

181

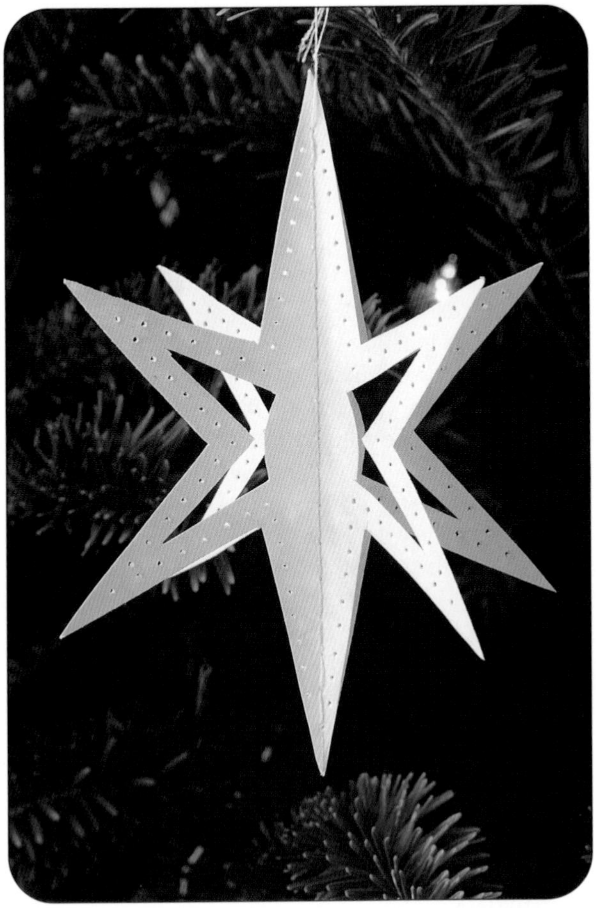

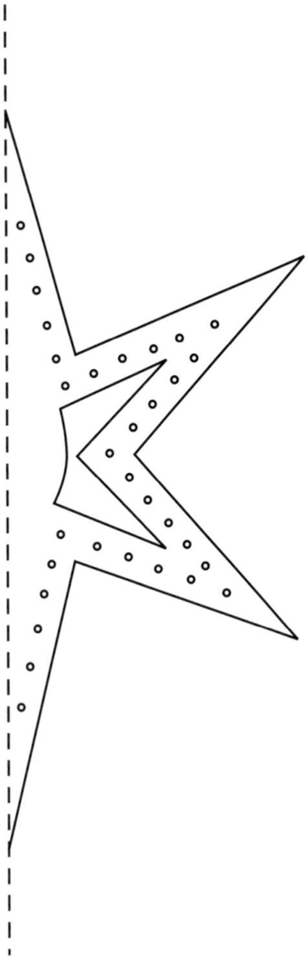

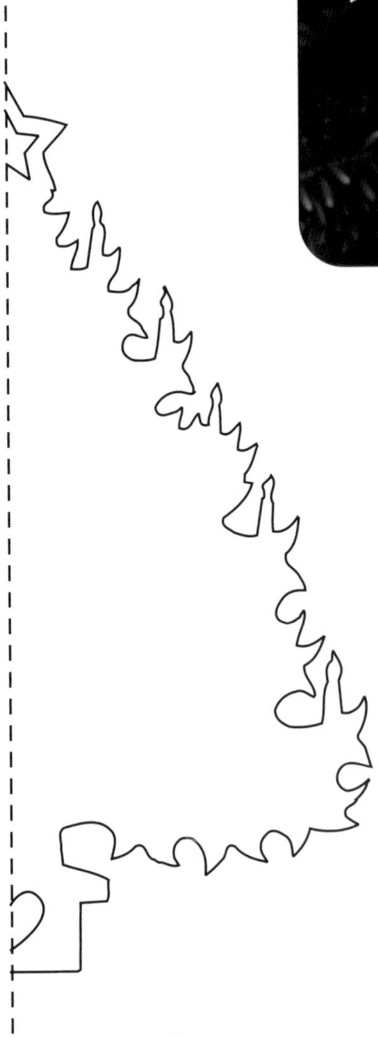

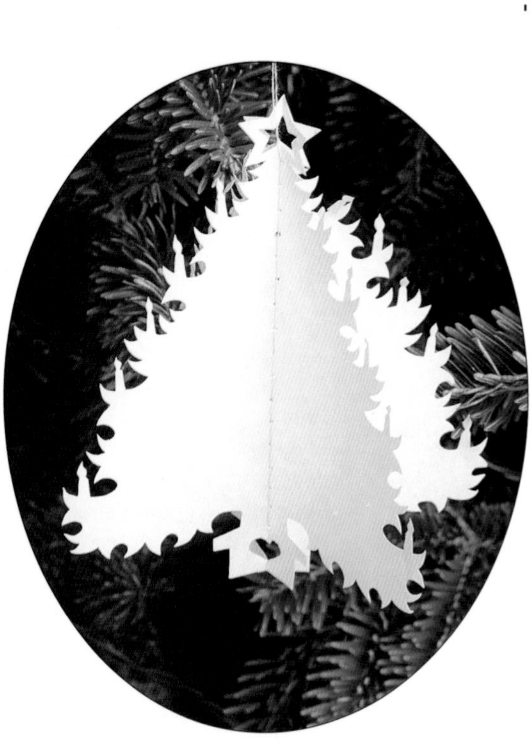

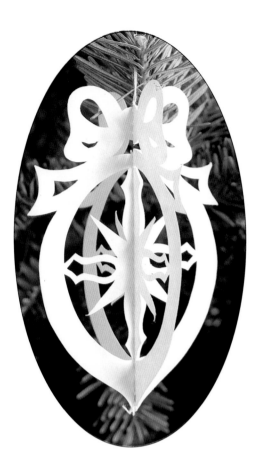

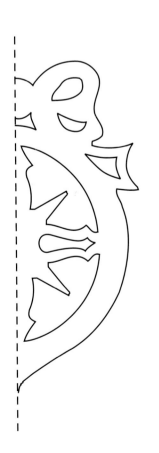

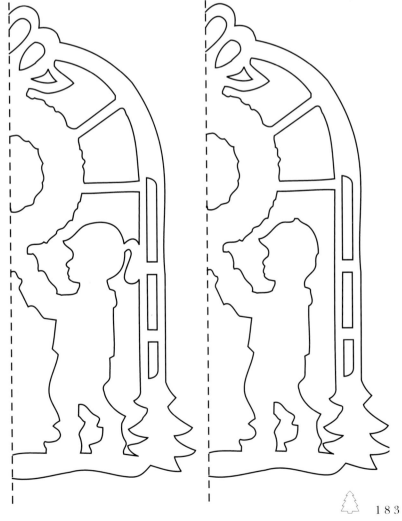

Why Evergreens Are Ever Green (Cherokee Version)

When all the trees on earth were newly made, the Great Spirit spoke to them. "I want you to stay awake and watch over the earth for seven nights," he said.

All the trees intended to obey. On the first night, everyone remained awake. The second night was harder, and just before dawn the sourwoods nodded off. On the third night, the trees whispered to each other in the wind to keep themselves awake, but even so, the dogwoods dozed. On the fourth night the maples slept, on the fifth night, the beeches, and, on the sixth night, even the oaks. After seven nights only a few stalwart trees remained awake: the pine, the spruce, the fir, the cedar, the holly, and the laurel.

The Great Spirit was very pleased. "You have great strength," he said, "great loyalty. You shall be, for all time, the guardians of the forest."

Ever since then, while other trees lose their leaves and sleep through the long, cold winter, the evergreens stay awake, keeping watch over the earth.

✱ KIMONOS ✱

These simple paper ornaments are made from handsome marbled paper, but you can make them out of any decorative paper.

Materials

Marbled paper (or other decorative paper), scissors, rubber cement, thread for hanger

1. Cut two pieces of paper 3 inches by 4-1/2 inches (7.5 x 11 cm). Cut them from two different papers. In a third paper, cut one piece of paper 1/4 inch wide (6 mm) and 12 inches long (30 cm).

2. To make the arms, fold one piece of paper in half along its length. On the side without the fold, cut the paper into a gentle curve (see Figure 1). Glue the wrong sides of the arms together.

4. On one end of the body, cut along each fold 1-1/2 inches (4 cm). See Figure 3. Insert the arms into the slits. Glue the front of the body down flat.

5. Fold the long, narrow strip of paper in half, making a V-shaped fold (see Figure 4). Glue the folded strip to the front of the kimono, with just the V-shaped portion projecting above the kimono.

6. When the glue has dried, cut the kimono level at the bottom.

7. To make a hanger, loop a piece of thread through the V and knot the ends.

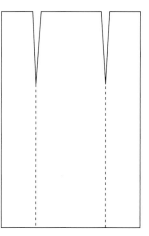

FIGURE 3

FOLD

CUT

FIGURE 1

3. To make the body, fold the second piece of paper 3/4 inch (19 mm) from each long edge. The edges of the folded paper should meet in the center (see Figure 2).

FIGURE 4

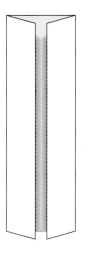

FIGURE 2

If Not a Christmas Tree...

Pines are also put to other, less seasonal uses. Able to grow on dry, sandy soils that would support few other crops, pines are probably the most important timber trees in the world and a major source of paper. In Germany and Sweden the needles are treated to remove the resin and soften the fibers; the resultant "forest wool" is woven into garments and stuffed into cushions and mattresses.

❀ PAPER DOILY TREE ❀

Inexpensive paper doilies serve as candleholders and tree toppers on this child-friendly tree. Bright cellophane lollipops and spicy gingerbread people add old-fashioned touches. When used as tree ornaments, gingerbread people need to be considerably hardier than when they're designed for eating. The recipe below makes some tough cookies to trim your tree.

Paper Doily Candleholders

Materials

Lacy paper doily, red "birthday" candle, white chenille craft stem, red and white ribbons 1/4 inch (6 mm) wide

1. Place the candle somewhat off center on the doily and gather the doily up around the bottom of the candle. The shorter side of the doily will be the front of the ornament, with the higher section in back.
2. Twist the chenille stem twice around the doily-wrapped candle, leaving a piece of stem free on each end.
3. Form a bow with the red and white ribbons and wrap the chenille stem ends around it. Use the remaining ends of the chenille stem to wire the ornament to the tree.

Gingerbread People

1 cup (235 g) margarine, softened
3/4 cup (135 g) firmly packed brown
    sugar
1/2 cup (90 g) granulated sugar
1/3 cup (80 ml) molasses
3/4 cup (175 ml) dark corn syrup
3 eggs
8-1/2 cups (1 kg) all-purpose flour
1 tablespoon baking soda
1 teaspoon salt
1 teaspoon *each* ground ginger,
    cloves, allspice, and cinnamon

Cream margarine and both sugars together. Add molasses, corn syrup, and eggs, and beat until smooth. Stir together the flour, baking soda, salt, and spices, and stir the dry mixture into the wet one. Divide the dough into two balls, cover with plastic wrap, and refrigerate two hours.

Preheat the oven to 350°F (176°C). Roll one ball of the chilled dough about 1/4 inch thick (6 mm), using a

floured rolling pin. With a cookie cutter, cut out as many gingerbread people as the size of your cutter will allow.

Transfer the cookies to a lightly greased baking sheet. Cut a hole for a hanger, using the end of a plastic drinking straw. Bake 10 to 12 minutes or until lightly browned. Place on wire rack to cool.

Thread a piece of narrow red ribbon through the hole to serve as a hanger, and tie a white ribbon bow around the neck.

Cellophane Lollipops

Materials

Foam ball 1 inch (2.5 cm) in diameter, craft pick, low-melt glue gun, colored cellophane, narrow ribbon

1. Glue the end of the craft pick to the center of the foam ball.
2. Wrap a piece of cellophane around the lollipop and tie it up with narrow ribbon.

Paper Doily Tree Topper

Materials

2 dozen paper doilies (or more or less, depending upon how large a tree you need to top), floral wire, narrow red ribbon, white glue

1. Gather a doily in the center, creating a cone with lace edges. Wire the doily around the center, leaving wire tails about 10 inches (25 cm) long.
2. Repeat with the remaining doilies.
3. Gather all the wire ends together, forming a huge "bouquet" of doilies. Insert the ends of the red ribbons down into the center of the bouquet. Twist the wires around each other.
4. To attach the topper to the tree, wrap the wires around a central upright spike.

The Selling of the Christmas Tree (Media Version)

In 1848 the *Illustrated London News* appeared with a charming drawing on the cover: Queen Victoria, Prince Albert (a German-born prince), and their many children gathered around a Christmas tree. The British public was enchanted, and the Christmas tree acquired a certain respectability.

Two years later, *Godey's Lady's Book*, an influential American periodical, printed the same drawing, tactfully erasing the queenly tiara and avoiding any mention of a royal family. Americans were delighted, and the Christmas tree gained wider currency.

✄ PAPER PINWHEELS ✄

Each pinwheel shown in the photo
was made with two pieces of decorative
paper: one marbled and one metallic.
Any two sheets of pretty paper will
work, as long as at least one of them
has considerable body.

Materials

White glue (preferably one that remains flexible when it dries), 2 4-inch (10 cm) squares of decorative paper, waxed paper, ice pick, scissors, round-nosed jewelry pliers (or needle-nosed pliers), 2-inch (5 cm) length of 20-gauge jewelry wire (or other heavy-gauge wire), 2 small beads

1. Wrong sides together, glue the decorative papers together. Sandwich them between two sheets of waxed paper and weigh them down with a large, heavy book until dry.
2. Cut the glued papers into a 3-1/2-inch (9 cm) square.
3. Pencil a pale line diagonally between each set of opposite corners.
4. With an ice pick or similar tool, punch a hole where the two lines intersect.
5. On the left side of each quadrant, punch a small hole 1/8 inch (1.5 cm) from the point (see Figure 1).
6. Starting at the edges of the square, cut along each diagonal line, stopping 1/4 inch (6 mm) from the center.
7. With the pliers, bend one end of the wire into a closed loop.
8. Slip a small bead over the other end of the wire until it rests on the loop.
9. Slip the wire through the center hole in the square, going from the paper you want on the outside of the pinwheel to the paper you want on the inside.
10. Bring one corner of the paper toward the center and insert the wire through the hole. Bring the next adjacent corner to the center, then the next, then the last one, inserting the wire in each hole (see Figure 2).

11. Add the other bead to the wire.
12. Compress the center of the pinwheel and clip the wire about 3/8 inch (1 cm) from the top bead. Use the pliers to bend the wire end into a loop.
13. To form a hanger, punch a small hole in one wing tip, thread a piece of colored string through the hole, and knot the ends.

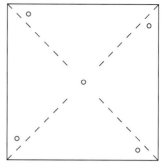

FIGURE 1

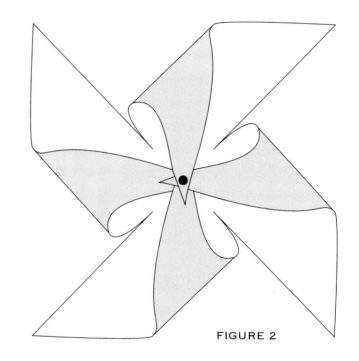

FIGURE 2

Christmas Lights

In 1882 Edward Johnson, a friend and cohort of Thomas Edison, invented electric Christmas tree lights: egg-sized globes of red, white, and blue. The bulbs were sold individually, each on a separate wire, and were prohibitively expensive for most people. After the turn of the century, economical strings of lights appeared.

Cones, Pods
& Grasses

❄ CORNHUSK CAROLERS ❄

In the fall, cornhusks are available in most craft shops and discount marts with craft departments. Despite the apparent sophistication of these singing angels, they are not difficult to make.

Materials

2 ounces (60 g) of cornhusks; heavy-, medium-, and fine-gauge floral wire; 3/4-inch-diameter (2 cm) foam ball; dried cornsilk; white glue; glue gun; masking tape

1. Soak the cornhusks in a bucket of warm water for 15 to 30 minutes, until they're easy to bend and fold. (If you have trouble separating packaged cornhusks, just put the whole bundle in the bucket for a few minutes.)

2. Cut a 3-inch (8 cm) piece of heavy wire and make a fish hook in one end. Insert the other end into the foam ball.

3. Cut a piece of cornhusk about 2 inches (5 cm) wide and 5 inches (12 cm) long. Gather it in the middle. Place it on top of the ball and pull the wire until the hook is all the way into the foam, trapping the gathered husk in the center and fastening it to the ball. See Figure 1. Spread the husk over the ball to cover it; you now have the head. Twist a piece of fine-gauge wire around the neck. See Figure 2.

4. Now for the arms. Cut a 6-inch (15 cm) piece of medium-gauge wire and place it lengthwise along one side of a cornhusk that's about 7 inches (18 cm) long and 3 inches (4 cm) wide. Roll the husk snugly around the wire. Tie the center of this cylinder with fine-gauge wire. Trim the husk ends so the cylinder is

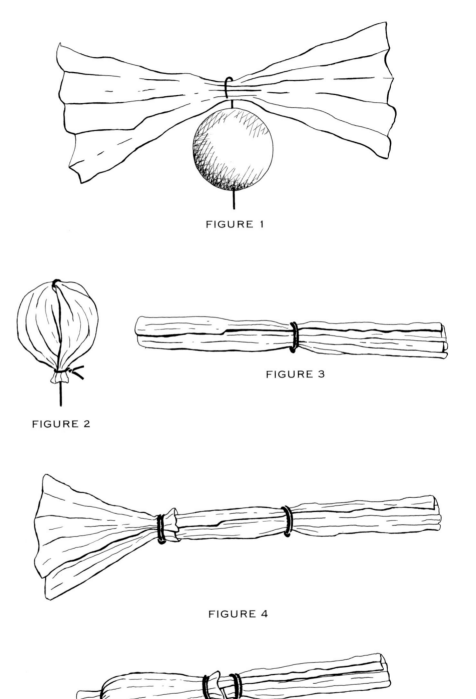

FIGURE 1

FIGURE 2

FIGURE 3

FIGURE 4

FIGURE 5

6 inches (15 cm) long. See Figure 3.

5. To make the sleeves, gather a 3-inch square of cornhusk around one arm about 1/2 inch (1 cm) from one end and tie it with fine wire. See Figure 4. Turn the husk inside out, back toward the center of the cylinder. Tie the sleeve at the center of the arm with fine wire. See Figure 5. Repeat on the other side to make the other sleeve.

6. Position the arms an appropriate distance below the head and wire them to the center "backbone" wire.

7. For the bodice, cut two pieces of husk 1-1/4 inches (3 cm) wide and about 3 inches long. To avoid unfinished edges, fold each long side to the center, so that each strip is 3/4 inch wide. Lay the center of each strip on a shoulder and bring the ends down the front and back, crossing at the waist in both front and back. Wrap a piece of fine wire around the waist and twist the wire ends together.

8. To make the skirt, first bend the arms up out of your way. Using your largest and best-looking husk first, place four to six large husks evenly around the chest and head, overlapping the waist by about 1/2 inch. See Figure 6. Wrap a piece of fine wire around the waist and fold the skirt down. Trim the bottom of the skirt to make it even.

9. Reposition the arms while they're still wet, arranging them so the angel will be ready to hold sheet music. Allow to dry completely, about four days.

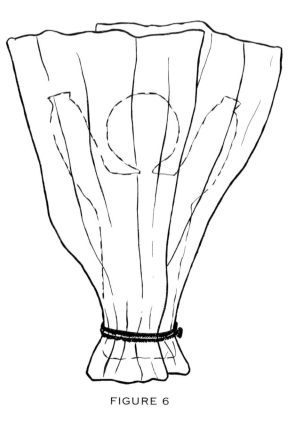

FIGURE 6

10. For angel hair, spread white glue on the head and wrap the cornsilk around the head. Glue down (or trim) any flyaway silks; no angel should have a bad hair day.

11. Glue two large husks together to make one thick one, using craft glue, and allow to dry. Cut out a pair of wings and some sheet music and hot-glue them to the usual places.

12. Cut a 2-inch piece of heavy-gauge wire and wrap it with masking tape. Bend it into a halo and insert it into the back of the head.

❈ PINECONE TREE ❈

An enormous cone from a sugar pine serves as a miniature Christmas tree.

Materials

Pinecone about 12 inches (30 cm) tall; 6-inch (15 cm) vine wreath base; heavy-gauge floral wire; 4 feet (1.2 m) of miniature artificial pine garland; 4 feet of gold bead garland; metallic gold wired ribbon 1/16 inch (1.5 mm) wide; white spray paint; 25 to 30 pinecones 1/2 inch to 1 inch wide (1 to 3 cm); 3 large, red, artificial berries; miniature packages; 3 sprays of small, red, artificial berries

1. Fold a piece of heavy-gauge floral wire loosely in half and slip it around the cone between the two bottom rows of petals. Pull the wire tight against the center of the cone. Wire the cone twice more, positioning the wire ends in different places.
2. Using the wire ends, wire the cone to the vine base.
3. Spiral the pine garland and the gold bead garland down the length of the cone. To begin, wire them to the top of the cone; to end, hot-glue them to the wreath base.
4. Make 10 two-loop bows of the wired gold ribbon and wire them to the garland.
5. Spray the small pinecones white and allow them to dry. Hot-glue them randomly around the large cone.
6. Make a bow of beaded gold garland and one of wired gold ribbon, and glue or wire them to the top of the tree. Hot-glue the large red berries to the center of the bow.
7. Hot-glue the miniature packages around the base of the tree. Dress the packages up by hot-gluing small berries or cones to them. Hot-glue sprays of artificial berries between the packages.

❋ CONE CORSAGE ❋

In this ornament from nature, each component is attached to floral wire and then wired to the other items.

Materials

Cone or cone flower, 3 nutshell segments, floral wire, brown floral tape, narrow red ribbon

1. Wire a nutshell segment by holding it against a 5-inch (12 cm) piece of floral wire, toward the end of the wire, and wrapping brown floral tape around both shell and wire. The wrapped part of the shell will show, adding a two-tone design element, so make it a clean wrap. Continue to spiral the tape up the wire until the entire length is wrapped. Repeat for the remaining nutshells.

2. Wrap an 8-inch (20 cm) piece of floral wire with brown floral tape. Fold the wire loosely in half and slip it around the cone, between the two bottom rows of petals. Pull the wire tight against the center of the cone, and twist the wire ends together right next to the cone.

3. Make a six- or eight-loop bow from narrow red velvet ribbon and wire it around the center with a 4-inch (10 cm) piece of wire that you've wrapped with brown floral tape.

4. To assemble the ornament, first secure the three nutshell pieces in a V shape by taping around all three wires, taping their full lengths.

5. Position the cone at the top of the nutshells, with its wire pointing away from the nuts. Tape around its wire and the nutshell wires.

6. Shape the wrapped wires into a spiral-curving stem and cut any excess tape off the end of the stem.

7. Position the bow just behind the cone and twist its wires around the stem. Use the wire ends from the bow to attach the ornament to the tree.

⁂ Carved Gourds ⁂

To make a spectacular carved ornament, you need only a seasoned gourd (see "Gourds of the Season" on page 84), some leather dye, brown shoe polish, and a wood gouge. Look for U-shaped gouges (not the straight-edged or V-shaped ones) in a variety of small sizes wherever woodcarving tools are sold. The carved areas on a gourd are more porous than the uncarved shell and will dye a darker color.

Two-Color Gourd

Materials

Seasoned gourd, soft lead pencil, U-shaped gouge, brown leather dye, brown paste wax shoe polish, clean cloths, awl, decorative cord

1. Sketch your design on a piece of scratch paper; then pencil the design on the gourd.
2. Gouge out the appropriate areas, using different sizes of gouges as needed.

   To make clean cuts, first hold the gouge at a right angle to the gourd and make a stop cut. Then, holding the gouge at a low angle, shave a chip out of the surface, aiming toward the stop cut and stopping there (see Figure 1). Continue gouging out chips until the pattern is complete.
3. Rub brown leather dye over the entire gourd, using a clean rag. Wipe off the excess with a second rag. The dye will turn the carved areas a dark brown and the uncarved areas a medium to deep tan. Since each gourd takes the color differently, the shades of your ornaments will vary. Allow to dry.
4. Using a soft rag, rub paste wax shoe polish over the entire gourd to give it a natural-looking shine.
5. Using the awl, make a small hole through the stem for the hanger.
6. Thread the decorative cord through the hole and tie the ends in a bow.

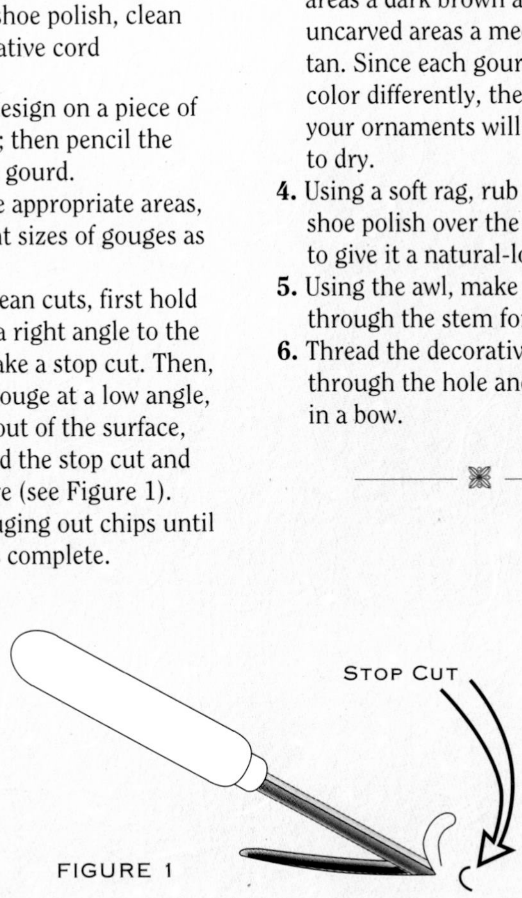

FIGURE 1

Long-Necked, Tri-Color Gourd

Materials

Same as for two-color gourd

1. Pencil the long, diagonal lines on the gourd.
2. Use a small gouge to carve out the lines you have drawn, creating an indentation along each one.
3. Decide which diamond shapes will be the darkest and gouge a series of chips from inside them. (Follow the above instructions for making clean cuts.)
4. With a clean rag, wipe brown leather dye over the carved triangles, then wipe if off with another rag. The dye will turn the porous gouged areas a dark brown and the uncarved areas a lighter color.
5. Rub brown paste wax shoe polish over the whole gourd and allow it to dry. Then gouge out the uncarved areas. The light-colored material underneath provides the pale third color.
6. Make a hanger as described above.

❊ PINE NEEDLE BROOM ORNAMENT ❊

Wherever pine trees grow, people have woven the fallen needles into baskets and other containers—yet another gift of the evergreen.

Materials

About 80 pine needle clusters, scissors, strong red thread, 4 twist ties, needle, acrylic spray, glue gun, various decorative materials

1. Soak the pine needles in hot water for 30 minutes, to make them pliable.
2. Make a bundle of 30 pine needle clusters, lining up the ends of the caps evenly.
3. Wrap a 12-inch (30 cm) piece of thread around the pine bundle just under the caps and tie a knot (see Figure 1). Knot the ends of the thread to form a hanger.

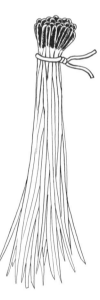

FIGURE 1

4. Make two bundles with 24 needle clusters each. Secure each bundle temporarily at both ends with the twist ties.
5. Separate the first bundle in half and insert the other two bundles into the opening, with the caps on one bundle to the right and the caps on the other bundle to the left. Push the two horizontal bundles up as far as possible.
6. Center a 30-inch (75 cm) piece of thread over the vertical bundle and wrap it twice around the

vertical bundle, right below the two horizontal bundles (see Figure 2). Knot the thread.

7. Thread the needle onto the right thread end. Bend the lower horizontal bundle down in an inverted U shape. Bring the needle around the right bundle and back through the middle bundle to secure (see Figure 3). Bring the needle around the left bundle and back through the center bundle.

8. Bend the top horizontal bundle down into an inverted U and sew it to the adjacent bundles in a similar fashion. Bring any loose threads to the front of the ornament and tie them off.

9. Cut the bottom of the broom off evenly and allow it to dry.

10. Spray the broom with clear acyclic.

11. Use the glue gun to attach small decorative materials. Shown, back row, left to right: red angel hair, hemlock cones, and greenery; pine petals and hemlock cone; white velvet bow, German statice, and tiny craft bird. Front row, left to right: dried greenery, raffia bow, hemlock cone flower; swiss straw bow, whitened cones, and red beads.

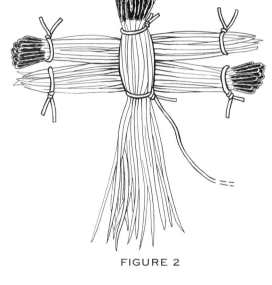

FIGURE 2

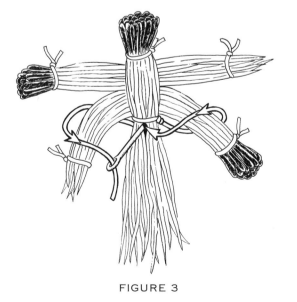

FIGURE 3

Pine Needles

Pine needles grow in bundles of two, three, or five. The bundles are held together and to the twig with a brown papery husk. Needles vary in length, from the 3/4-inch (2 cm) needles of the jack pine to the magnificent 18-inch (45 cm) needles of the longleaf pine so beloved by basket weavers. Each needle boasts a thick, waxy outer layer, or cuticle, that reduces the amount of moisture the tree loses and thus allows it to survive in areas that are too dry and cold for other species.

❋ BASKET TREE ❋

If you're an admirer of handmade baskets, why not turn your tree into a celebration of this fine craft? Miniature baskets abound. Wrap narrow red ribbon around the handles and finish with a bow at each end, or thread the ribbon through a large-eyed needle and weave the ribbon in and out of the basket itself.

And weave a few simple ornaments of your own: a woven square, a birdcage, a heart, and an Indian dream catcher. Reed (both round and flat) is available wherever basket-making supplies are sold, including most large craft stores.

Woven Square

Materials
12 inches (30 cm) of flat reed 5/8 inch (1.3 cm) wide, package of red fabric dye (optional), razor knife

1. If you want a two-color piece, cut the reed in half. Make up the fabric dye according to package instructions. Heat it to boiling, remove from the heat, and place half the reed in to soak. Remove it when it's slightly darker than you want. Rinse the dyed reed several times.
2. Soak the undyed reed in a pan of water for about 10 minutes. If the dyed reed has dried, soak it also, in a different pan.
3. Cut four pieces of reed about 2-1/2 inches (6 cm) long—two dyed and two undyed. Make your cuts at an angle.
4. Fold each piece in half and weave them together as shown in the photo, inserting the ends of each piece through the fold of another.

Birdcage

Materials
#0 round reed, small craft bird in nest, glue gun, narrow red ribbon

1. Soak all the reed in lukewarm water for 20 minutes.
2. Cut four 20-inch (50 cm) pieces of reed. These will be the ribs—the pieces that form the bottom and the sides of the birdcage. Place two ribs over the other two ribs at right angles, so they cross in the center.
3. The rest of the birdcage is *twined*, a simple but sophisticated-looking technique. Fold a 6-foot (1.8 m) piece of reed in half—this will be the *weaver*—and slip the folded middle around a horizontal group of ribs (see Figure 1). Bring both halves of the weaver around both ribs, so the two pieces of weaver cross on the other side of the ribs. Now take both pieces of the weaver around the other three pairs of ribs, crossing them over each other each time.

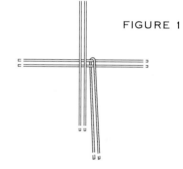

FIGURE 1

4. Go around the base a second time, twining around pairs of ribs (see Figure 2).
5. Now separate the pairs of ribs and twine loosely around the base one rib at a time (see Figure 3).

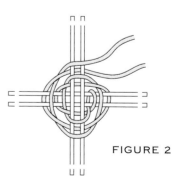

FIGURE 2

6. Continue to twine around the ribs, one at a time. As you work, shape the ribs upward to form the sides of the cage. Make sure the bottom is wide enough for the bird and nest.

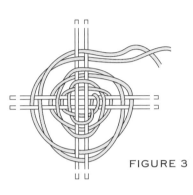

FIGURE 3

7. When you've twined two or three rows around the sides and the cage is taking shape, place the bird and nest in the center. Gather the ribs together at the top of the cage, and bring both ends of the weaver up to join them. Tie everything together with another piece of reed.
8. Tie a narrow red ribbon around the top of the cage.

———— ✖ ————

Heart

Materials
1 yard (90 cm) of 1/2-inch-wide (1.25 cm) paper-thin ash or thin, flexible reed, razor knife, white craft glue, alligator clips or mini clothespins, narrow red ribbon

1. Cut four pieces of ash 7-1/4 inches (18 cm) long. Cut each piece lengthwise into thirds. You should have 12 long, thin pieces. Discard two of them; you'll need a total of 10 for the heart.
2. Lay five pieces of ash vertically side by side.

3. Working toward one end of the group, weave a sixth piece horizontally over and under the first five (see Figure 1).

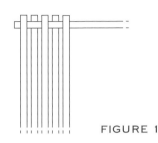

FIGURE 1

4. Weave another horizontal piece, alternating the vertical pieces it goes over and under. Weave the remaining pieces in similar fashion, making sure that no two adjacent weavers go over and under the same vertical piece (see Figure 2).

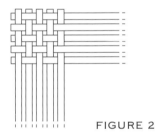

FIGURE 2

5. Tidy up the woven area to form a square, with the weavers parallel and the spaces between them about the same size.
6. Glue all intersections together. Place alligator clips at the edges to hold everything in place and allow to dry.
7. Turn the project with its point facing down toward you. Take the two outside strands, bring them toward the center, and cross the right one over the left (see Figure 3). Clip them together. Make sure you don't twist the weavers in the process; what was the top side on the glued section needs to be the top side in the clipped section.

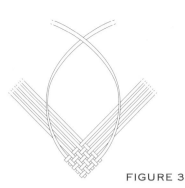

FIGURE 3

8. Take what are now the two outside strands and bring them toward the center. Bring the right one under the clipped end that points out to the right; weave the left one over and under the two ends (see Figure 4).
9. Again, take what are now the two outside weavers, and weave them over and under, making sure that they don't go over and under the same strands as their predecessors. Continue until all pieces of ash are woven.

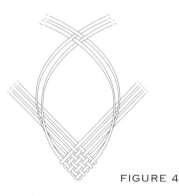

FIGURE 4

10. When all 10 ends are woven together—they should look like the first square you wove—tidy up the angles and glue all intersections together. Again, secure with clips until dry.
11. Fold the two ends of the piece together, point to point, and glue them together along the edges, from the points to about 1 inch (2.5 cm) up each side of the ornament. Clip and let dry.
12. Attach a bow and a hanger of red ribbon.

———— ✖ ————

Indian Dream Catcher

Materials

20 inches (50 cm) of #6 round reed or thin grapevine, 3-1/2 yards (3.3 m) of heavy, supple cord (leather thong or waxed linen, for example), feathers, beads

1. Make a 5-inch-diameter (12 cm) circle of round reed or vine. Tie the ends together with the cord or glue them together.
2. Tie a loop for hanging in one end of the cord. Then tie the cord onto the round base, about 3 inches (10 cm) from the hanging loop (see Figure 1).
3. The rest of the dream catcher is made with a series of loops. Move the cord about 2 inches (5 cm) to the right of where it's tied to the base and loop it around the base—that is, take the cord over the base, around behind it, and back to the front, bringing it, on that final step, through the loop it has formed (see Figure 1).
4. Make another loop 2 inches to the right, then another, and so on until the base is covered

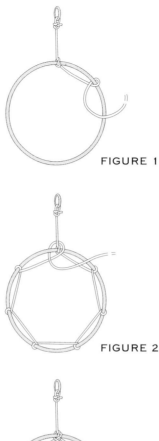

FIGURE 1

FIGURE 2

FIGURE 3

(see Figure 2).

Keep the cord taut as you work, but not so tight as to distort the circle. As you form each loop with your right hand, it's helpful to hold the previous loop with your left thumb and forefinger (the reverse if you're left-handed).

5. When you've been completely around the base, make the next loop in the center of the first straight string to your right. Continue around the circle in the same fashion, making a loop in the center of each straight piece of string (see Figure 3). Continue until the opening in the center is about 1 inch (2.5 cm) in diameter.
6. Many crafters finish at this point, knotting and cutting the string. Others continue with one final step. Loop around the innermost circle of string, placing the loops right next to each other and pulling each one tight. Cut the string close on the back of the project and fix it with a dot of glue.
7. For the hanging decoration, knot a piece of string at the bottom, thread onto it the beads of your choice, glue on a feather or two, and tie it to the bottom of the base.

Trimming the Tree

It's a yearly ritual: sawing off the bottom of the trunk until the Christmas tree stands level, only to discover that there's a huge gap in the foliage on one side. Sawing again, only to find a huge gap in the other side. Eventually you're down to a nub.

This is all less trying if the tree is a pine. Pine branches usually grow in whorls—more or less even layers—around the trunk, with one whorl added each year. Thus if you cut just below the branches on one side, you've probably cut just below the branches on all sides, leaving a decently symmetrical tree.

�֍ Seed Flower Ornaments ✖

Any attractive seeds can be used for these ornaments. Shown in the photo are pumpkin, cantaloupe, Japanese watermelon, striped sunflower, and Indian corn.

FIGURE 1

Materials
30 to 40 seeds, depending on size; 10 to 20 tiny seeds, such as rapeseed or white millet (common birdseed); 1-1/2-inch (4 cm) circle of thin cardboard or poster board, white craft glue; clear varnish spray; 5-inch (13 cm) length of heavy gold thread; 1-1/2-inch circle of felt

1. Lay a thin bead of glue around the edge of the cardboard circle.

2. Place the large seeds side by side around the circle, with about two-thirds of their length projecting out over the edge (see Figure 1). Allow the glue to dry.

3. Apply a circle of glue just below the seeds and add a second row of seeds, overlapping the first. Let dry. Apply a third row in the same way, overlapping the second.

4. Put a few drops of glue in the center of the ornament and add the tiny seeds, filling the space. Let dry.

5. Spray the ornament with clear varnish and allow it to dry.

6. Squeeze a circle of glue around the back of the ornament. To make a hanger, fold the gold thread in half and place the ends on the back. Glue on the felt.

✳ GOURD SANTAS ✳

You can turn small gourds into Santas that wear the colors and expressions of your choice.

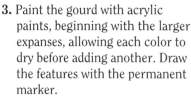

Materials

Seasoned gourd, soap, steel wool, soft lead pencil, acrylic paints, paintbrushes, black permanent marker, clear acrylic spray, awl or nail, long needle, embroidery floss

1. Soak the gourd in soapy water for half an hour, then scrub off all the dirt and mold with steel wool.
2. When the gourds are completely dry, sketch your design on the surface in pencil.
3. Paint the gourd with acrylic paints, beginning with the larger expanses, allowing each color to dry before adding another. Draw the features with the permanent marker.
4. When the paint is completely dry, spray the gourd with clear acrylic sealer.
5. Hold the Santa vertically and pencil dots on opposite sides of the stem. Using the awl or nail, punch a hole at each dot. Thread a long needle with embroidery floss and pass the needle through both holes. Knot the ends of the floss, forming a loop to serve as a hanger.

❈ ORNAMENTS FOR THE BIRDS ❈

In the dead of winter, birds need all the help they can get. These edible ornaments both decorate your yard and feed the birds, who will enter-tain you as they consume their Christmas dinner.

Materials
Large, attractive cone, peanut butter, wild birdseed, ribbon, floral wire

1. Turn the cone upside down and spread generous dollops of peanut butter on the petals. (For even better nutrition, combine equal parts of peanut butter and short-ening with a little cornmeal.)

2. Press wild birdseed into the gooey mixture.

3. Make a decorative bow from your favorite ribbon and wire it to the top of the ornament, leaving enough excess wire to form a generous loop for hanging.

❊ CONES AND FEATHERS ❊

If you have a collection of small mementos—toby mugs, for example—you can wire them to a Christmas tree, where everyone can enjoy them. Fill in with bows of red paper ribbon, purchased ornaments, and a few creations of your own.

Upright Cones

Materials: large, attractive pinecone, spring-close clothespin, glue gun

1. Hot-glue the bottom of the cone to the top of one arm of the clothespin. Allow to dry.
2. Clip the clothespin, cone and all, to a tree branch. Rather than hanging from the branch, as wired cones do, this cone will sit upright on top of the branch.

Feather Ornaments

Materials
White feather, gold spray paint, small spray of dried flowers, sweet gum ball, ribbon

1. Spray the feather lightly with gold paint and allow to dry.
2. Place the dried flowers and gum ball on the feather, with their stems pointing toward the quill end.
3. Tie the ribbon around the feather and both stems, holding the stems in place with the knot. Tie the ribbon in a bow.
4. Trim the stem ends of the flowers and gum ball.

Sweet Gum Balls

Materials
Sweet gum balls, gold spray paint, floral wire

1. Spray the gum balls lightly with gold paint. Allow to dry.
2. Using floral wire, wire the gum balls to the ends of the tree branches.

Firs

Unlike pines, which have round needles and hanging cones, firs have flat needles attached to the twig in sprays, and cones that sit erect on top of the branches. One of the handsomest of all conifers is the balsam fir. Shaped like an illustrator's fantasy of a Christmas tree, it holds its soft, flat, fragrant needles extremely well after it's cut. (In the wild, individual needles remain on the tree for an unusually long three to five years.) For years woods-men used the "Canada balsam" obtained from bark blisters as wound plasters, waterproof glue, and chewing gum.

Very similar is the Fraser fir, the preferred Christmas tree in much of the southern Unites States. Limited in range, it grows above 4,000 feet in the Appalachian Mountains.

The Douglas fir is native to the Pacific coasts of both Canada and the United States. When the western regions of those countries were being settled, the wood from Douglas firs supplied railroad ties, telegraph poles, and telephone poles that stretched for thousands of miles.

❋ GOURD BIRDHOUSES AND SEED GARLANDS ❋

What belongs in a tree? Birdhouses—or gourds decorated
to look like birdhouses—and garlands of gourd seeds.

Gourd Birdhouse

Materials

Seasoned gourd, brown paste wax shoe polish, black acrylic paint, paintbrush, awl, super glue, gourd stem or wooden matchstick

1. Soak the gourd in soapy water for 30 minutes, then use steel wool to scrub off all the dirt and mold. Allow to dry.
2. Using a soft rag, rub brown paste wax shoe polish over the gourd and allow it to dry.
3. Paint a doorway in black acrylic paint.
4. With a narrow awl, make a small hole below the door and superglue a length of gourd stem or wooden matchstick into the hole, to serve as a perch. Be careful not to let stray drops of glue fall on the gourd.

———— ✖ ————

Gourd Seed Garland

Materials

Gourd seeds, household bleach, red fabric dye, monofilament fishing line, large craft needle, ice pick (optional)

1. Clean all the flesh off the seeds and soak them for half an hour in a mixture of 1/2 cup (120 ml) household bleach to 1 quart (1 l) of water. Rinse the seeds in a colander.
2. Dye half the seeds red. In a two-quart (2 l) enamel or stainless steel pan, combine 2 cups (500 ml) water with 2 teaspoons powdered red fabric dye, and bring the mixture to a boil. Remove the dye from the heat and add the seeds. Let them sit for five to 10 minutes or until you like the color—keep in mind they'll be somewhat paler after they dry. Remove the seeds with a slotted spoon and spread them on newspaper to drain.
3. Reheat the dye and add the next batch of seeds, continuing the process until you've dyed as many seeds as want. If the dye weakens, add more powder.
4. Thread a piece of monofilament on the craft needle and knot the end. String the seeds while they're still wet, piercing them in the middle of a flat side. Alternate four red with four undyed seeds until the garland is the desired length. Knot the end of the thread and hang the garland to dry.

   Note: For easier stringing, pierce the seeds first with an ice pick.

✖ STRAW MARQUETRY ANGEL FACE ✖

An ancient art, straw marquetry involves using pieces of split straw as an applique. The most common is wheat straw—the long, hollow stalks that support the seed-bearing heads. If you live near a friendly wheat grower, ask to harvest a few handfuls, cutting it off near the ground. If not, wheat is available at many craft stores.

Materials

Wheat straw, craft knife, iron, sturdy paper (for example, a manila file folder), white craft glue, scissors

1. Cut off any attached seedheads and soak the straws in a mixture of three parts warm water to one part vinegar. (Vinegar helps to break down the starch in the straw.) How long the straw needs to soak can vary from 15 minutes to four hours, depending on the variety. If the supplier doesn't recommend a time, soak it until it's pliable. To test it, pinch the very end of the straw. If it springs back to your touch, it's ready.
2. With the craft knife, slit each straw down its full length and open it up. Iron the straw from the inside until it's flat and dry, being careful not to use an iron so hot that it scorches the straw. (Try permanent press.) Ironing will be easier if the straw doesn't rest on too soft a surface.
3. Transfer the patterns to sturdy paper and cut out the pieces. Be sure to cut *two complete wing sets*—two wing caps and two sets of feathers—and to flip one wing cap over when you add the straw splits, so your angel will have both right and left wings.

4. Apply glue to a pattern piece. Then cover it completely with straw splits, laying them side by side, shiny side up. All the straws on a pattern piece should be parallel. Make sure there aren't any gaps. Press the splits flat to the paper with your fingers or a burnishing tool.

5. After the glue is dry, turn the piece to the back and trim the straw ends with scissors, following the outline of the paper. To make the feathers look more featherlike, make 1/4-inch (6 mm) cuts around the edges (see the pattern).

6. Using the photo as a guide, glue the parts of the angel together. Start with the base as the bottom layer. Glue the feathers to the base one at a time, starting at the center and working outward on each side. Add the wing caps, then (in order) the face, hair, and halo.

(Pattern continued on next page.)

PATTERN

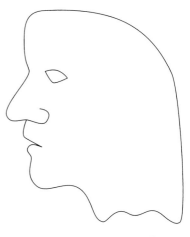

FACE

 215

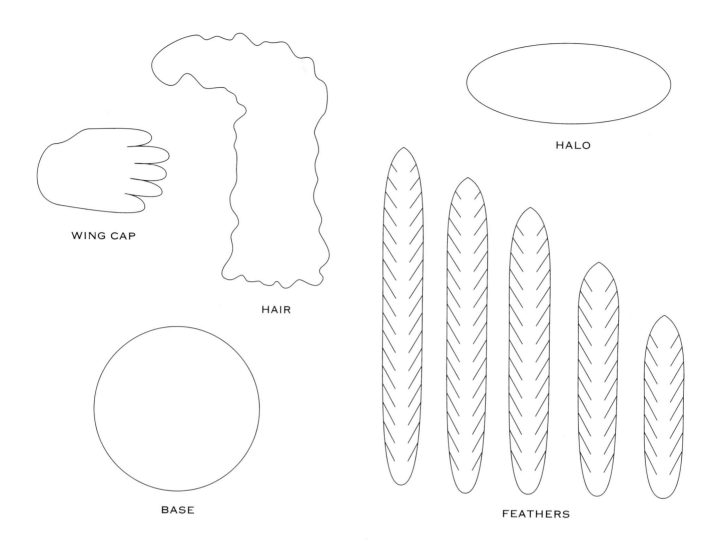

WING CAP

HAIR

HALO

BASE

FEATHERS

Spruces

Spruces are sharply conical evergreens with stiff, sharp, four-sided needles that grow singly all the way around the twigs. Their colors range from dark green to undeniably blue. (The ornaments on page 45 are shown on a blue spruce.) Spruces are a hardy bunch, growing north to the limit of trees, extending well into the sub-arctic tundra. Their soft, light wood is prized as sounding boards for pianos and for boat building. Although their needles drop rather quickly when dry, spruces are widely valued as Christmas trees. Some spruce lovers speculate that the tree's natty appearance explains the complimentary "all spruced up."

⚹ Australian Pine Cone Wreath ⚹

Huge trees with long, graceful needles, Australian pines produce tiny cones.

Materials

9-inch (22 cm) piece and 18-inch (45 cm) piece of heavy-gauge floral wire, brown floral tape, drill with 1/16-inch (1.5 mm) bit, 15 Australian pine cones, cotton pod, narrow red ribbon, clear acrylic spray

1. Wrap both pieces of wire with floral tape.
2. Drill a hole crosswise through each cone.
3. String the cones on the 18-inch piece of wire.
4. Bend the wire into a circle about 3 inches (7 cm) in diameter and twist the ends around each other, then into a small loop.
5. Wrap the 9-inch piece of wire around the cotton pod and attach it to the wreath, opposite the loop.
6. Spray the wreath lightly with clear acrylic sealer.
7. Attach a hanger of narrow red ribbon.

✳ WHEAT ORNAMENTS ✳

The rich beige tones of wheat look stunning against a dark evergreen.

Materials
Floral wire, wheat, ribbon, decorative pod and glue gun (optional)

1. Wire the stalks of wheat together just below the seedheads.
2. Make a full bow and wire it together around the center, leaving long wire ends. Wire the bow to the wheat.
3. If you like, you can hot-glue a decorative pod to the center of the bow.
4. Use the wire ends to attach the ornament to the tree.

✳ WHEAT TREE TOPPER ✳

Wire the long stalks of wheat vertically to the center of the tree—either on the back of the tree, so the fanned wheat bursts star-like from the top of the tree, or to the front, so that the long stalks are visible.

Materials

About 60 stalks of wheat 18 to 20 inches (45 to 50 cm) long, floral wire, glue gun, short stalks of wheat, ribbon, German statice, paper or cornhusk flower (optional)

1. Soak the wheat in warm water for about 1 hour, or until it's flexible enough to bend.
2. Lay the stalks of wheat together in a bundle with their tops even, and wire them together about 3 inches (7 cm) below the bottom of the seedheads. Spread the seedheads out in a fan shape.
3. Hot-glue short stalks of wheat to the back of the fan as necessary to make a full ornament, with their stalks in the center and their seeds fanning out.
4. Make a large, multi-loop bow and wire it on top of the other wire.
5. Hot-glue sprigs of German statice into the bow; the bow should look well filled, and you should use a lot of statice.
6. If desired, hot-glue a paper or corn-husk flower in the center of the bow.

Edible Evergreens

Conifers are fine food sources for wildlife. Once a cone releases the seeds it's been protecting, the feast is on. (Hence the need, from the tree's point of view, for protection.) Bears, coyotes, rabbits, squirrels, chipmunks, grouse, pheasants, and quail eat the fat- and protein-rich seeds of the local species, and humans nibble on the nuts from pinyon pines. Deer, moose, squirrels, and rabbits browse on the branches, and porcupines gnaw on the bark.

Edibles

✳ CANDY GARLAND ✳

Eat one, string two—the best formula for making colorful garlands out of dimestore candy.

Materials
Candy, strong craft needle 2 to 3 inches (5 to 8 cm) long, strong thread, glue gun, jute cord

1. If the candy has convenient holes or can be pierced with a needle, just string it as you would cranberries and popcorn, using the needle and a doubled thread. This technique works fine for the red licorice pieces, giant gumdrops, multicolored licorice, and gummy rings pictured here. Just be prepared to wipe sticky candy off the needle regularly.
2. If the candy can't be strung—hard candy can't be, and some gummy candies crack and break—it can be hot-glued to a piece of heavy jute cord with a low-melt glue gun. The Swedish fish and blue sharks pictured are attached that way, as are the peppermint circles and sour cherry balls.

FRONTIER CHRISTMAS

Combine a rustic log cabin...some prickly wreaths made from sycamore pods...old-fashioned popcorn balls and gingerbread...a tree topper of rough-woven burlap—and you have the makings of a tree that celebrates the do-it-yourself, make-your-own-fun frontier spirit. Fill in with simple bows of paper ribbon, tied or wired to the branches, and sprigs of German statice placed randomly around the tree. For the gingerbread figures, see the recipe on page 65.

Log Cabin

Materials

8-1/2- by 11-inch (21 X 27 cm) manila folder or other lightweight cardboard, scissors, craft cement or white glue, light brown spray color, straight pretzels about 2-1/2 inches (6 cm) long, oyster crackers, awl or large nail, craft pick or toothpick, heavy string, bite-size frosted shredded wheat cereal, black acrylic paint, small flat paintbrushes, acrylic spray

1. Enlarge the pattern or use it as a guide to draw your own. Each wall should be no more than 2-1/2 inches wide (so the pretzels will fit). Height is optional. Cut the cabin out of the manila folder. Fold on the fold lines, overlap the walls and tabs, and glue the cabin together. Allow to dry.
2. Cut a rectangle about 3-1/2 by 5 inches (9 X 13 cm) from the manila folder for the roof.
3. Lightly spray cabin (inside and out) and one side of the roof with light brown spray—for example, floral sandalwood color.
4. Glue the pretzels to the walls, beginning at the bottom and cutting them to fit (see Figure 1).
5. Glue one or two pretzels vertically at each corner, to fill the space and cover the cardboard.
6. Matching the short edges, fold the roof in half. Rest the roof on the cabin's roof line tabs, and glue it to the cabin. Allow to dry.

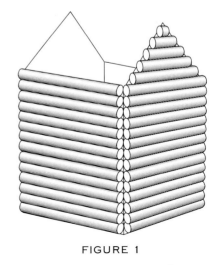

FIGURE 1

Photocopy pattern at 285%.

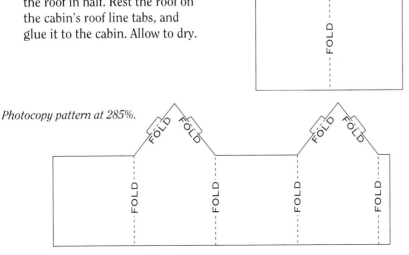

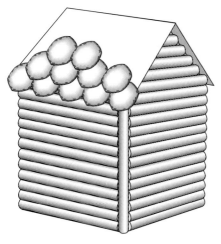

FIGURE 2

7. Using the awl or nail, punch a small hole in the center of the roof. Tie an 18-inch (45 cm) piece of string to the center of the floral pick, and thread the other end of the string through the hole, inside to outside. This will serve as the ornament's hanger. The floral pick should fit into the long fold of the roof and provide extra support.

8. To shingle the roof, glue a row of oyster crackers along the bottom of each side of the roof. Allow that row to dry, then another row, staggering and overlapping the second row. Allow to dry, then repeat until the roof is covered (see Figure 2).

9. To make the chimney, glue two pieces of shredded wheat to the roof.

10. Paint the windows and door, using black acrylic paint.

11. Apply two coats of acrylic spray, allowing time to dry between coats.

———— ✖ ————

Sycamore Wreaths

Materials

Glue gun, sycamore balls or sweet gum balls, German statice, nandina berries or other firm, red berries

1. Hot-glue the sycamore balls to each other to form a circle. Allow the glue to dry.
2. Hot-glue sprigs of German statice and nandina berries evenly around the wreaths.

———— ✖ ————

Popcorn Balls

Makes 6-8 balls

1/4 cup (25 g) margarine or butter
1/2 cup (120 ml) light corn syrup
1/2 cup sugar
1/2 teaspoon salt
8 cups (2 l) popped corn
Yellow cellophane
Heavy string

1. In a very large (about 4-quart, or 4-l) pot, heat margarine, corn syrup, sugar, and salt over medium-high heat, stirring constantly until sugar is dissolved.
2. Add popped corn and cook, stirring constantly, until all the popcorn is coated, about 3 minutes. Allow to cool just until comfortable to touch (don't let it harden).
3. Wet your hands, and shape the popcorn into balls about 3 inches (8 cm) in diameter. Place balls on waxed paper and allow to cool completely.
4. Wrap each ball in yellow cellophane, twist closed, and tie with string, leaving a long enough tail to tie to the tree.

———— ✖ ————

Moon and Star Tree Topper

2 pieces of brown burlap about 14 inches (35 cm) square (for the moon), 2 pieces of white burlap about 6 inches (15 cm) square (for each star), fiberfill, glue gun, fabric paint or marker, monofilament fishing line, 10-inch (25 cm) piece of medium-gauge wire

1. Using the pattern below as a guide, draw a moon about 12 inches (30 cm) tall. Cut out the pattern.
2. Lay the two large squares of burlap on top of each other. Pin the pattern to the pieces of burlap, and cut out two moons.
3. Hot-glue them together around the edges, about 1/2 inch (1 cm) in from the edge, leaving an opening about 2 inches (5 cm) long. Allow the glue to dry.
4. Stuff the moon with the fiberfill, then glue the opening closed.
5. Use fabric paint or marker to shade cheeks. If necessary, trim any rough edges of fabric.
6. Make the star by the same method.
7. With the monofilament, hang the star from the moon.
8. On the back side of the moon, thread the wire into and back out of the burlap, and wire the ornament to the tree.

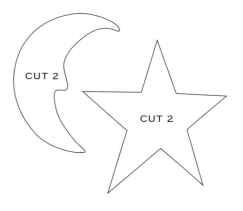

CUT 2

CUT 2

✳ FRUIT TABLE TREE ✳

Want to make the kids happy? Take the apples and oranges back out of their stockings, put the fruit on a Christmas tree, and put a lot of too-sweet, nutrition-free candy in the stockings.

Materials
Artificial tree about 25 inches (63 cm) tall, 16-inch-square (40 cm) cloth napkin, heavy string, sprigs of dried mountain mint (or other large, firm-leaved herb), dried apple slices, preserved orange slices, 10 dried pomegranates

1. Gather the napkin around the base of the tree and tie it around the trunk with string. Fold the edges of the napkin over to hide the string.
2. Hot-glue sprigs of mint to as many branch ends as possible.
3. Hot-glue the apple and orange slices to the tips of tree branches, positioning them randomly around the tree.
4. Hot-glue the pomegranates to the tree. Since they're heavier than the other fruit, position them closer to the tree trunk.

✳ ORANGE-FILLED ORNAMENTS ✳

The scent of citrus is as much a part of Christmas as the fragrance of evergreens.

Materials
3-inch-diameter (8 cm) plastic pot-pourri ornament, 1/4 cup (60 ml) dried orange granules, glue gun, 2 preserved orange slices, 2 1-inch (2.5 cm) cinnamon sticks, 2 bay leaves, whole star anise, raffia

1. Place the orange granules in the ornament and close it securely.
2. Using the photo as a guide, hot-glue the bay leaves in place.
3. Hot-glue a whole orange slice over the junction of the bay leaves. Cut the remaining orange slice in half and glue the halves on either side of the whole slice, tucking the straight edges under slightly.
4. Hot-glue the cinnamon sticks over the bay leaves and under the half slices.
5. Hot-glue the star anise in the center of the whole orange slice.
6. Make a raffia loop for a hanger and tie it to the ornament's plastic loop. Make a raffia bow and tie it to the bottom of the hanger.

❈ PASTA E FAGIOLI ❈

One of the best-loved winter soups in the world, *pasta e fagioli* ("pasta fah-ZOOL," sort of) is a gift from the good cooks of Italy. The pasta-and-bean soup is so warming and comforting on a raw December night that a Christmas tree in its honor is not too extravagant a gesture.

Pasta Ornaments

Materials

Dried pasta, glue, ribbon or decorative cord

1. Arrange the pasta into interesting patterns and glue it together, using the glue of your choice. Tacky glue works well, and it dries clear and virtually invisible, even though you need a substantial bead to hold two pieces together. Hot-glue is easy to apply and holds the pieces very securely, but it tends to show if you're not careful.
2. Glue a ribbon hanger to the back of the ornament or tie it to a handy portion.

--- ❈ ---

Bean Balls

Materials

Satin balls, dried beans, glue gun, glitter glue sticks, clear acrylic spray, decorative cord

1. Beans are fairly heavy, so the smaller balls are better than the large ones. Working from the top down, apply hot glitter glue to a section of the ball and press the beans one at a time into the glue. Use various types and colors of beans to make designs.
2. Spray the finished ornament with clear acrylic.
3. Hot-glue a loop of decorative cord to the top as a hanger.

✳ OKRA ✳

An African native, okra has been introduced to the other parts of the world by African immigrants who carried the seeds and the cooking methods with them. Okra is good fried, stewed, or painted.

Materials
Whole okra pods, acrylic paints, paint-brush, glitter (optional), clear varnish spray, embroidery floss, glue gun

1. Place the okra in a warm, moisture-free place to dry for about two months.
2. Paint the pods. If desired, dust a few of them with fine glitter while the paint is still wet.

3. When the okra are completely dry, spray them with clear varnish.
4. Hot-glue a loop of embroidery floss to each stem to form a hanger.

Cinnamon Santas

The scent of cinnamon is a pleasant addition to a Christmas tree.

Materials
Cinnamon stick about 6 inches (15 cm) long, 2 cinnamon sticks 2-1/2 to 3 inches (6 to 8 cm) long, glue gun, acrylic paints, tiny cotton ball, red ribbon 1/16 inch (1.5 mm) wide for hanger

1. On the bottom of the two short cinnamon sticks—the "arms"—paint red and white cuffs.
2. Paint a Santa face and a red hat on the long cinnamon stick.
3. Hot-glue the cinnamon sticks together, with the long one in the center.
4. Make a loop of the red ribbon and glue it to the top of the "head." Glue a cotton ball to the hat.

Pet Safety

Pets will eat anything, including things that will harm them. Metal ornament hooks can stick in their throats, and long pieces of string, yarn, tinsel, or cellophane can get stuck in the twists and turns of their intestines. The first canine who pigged out on chocolate is probably responsible for the phrase "sick as a dog."

If you have a curious and chronically hungry pet (two redundancies right there), you might forgo any food-based ornaments. Even if the food itself isn't harmful, your pet may get into other trouble while it's foraging.

Strawberry Corn

With its rich, red color and endearing size, strawberry corn is a fine ornamental for Christmas crafting. Widely available as seed corn for the home garden or as full-grown ears in the fall, strawberry corn normally grows a mere 2 to 3 inches (5 to 8 cm) long.

White Ornament

Materials: ear of strawberry corn, gold spray paint, decorative gold cord, glue gun, dusty miller leaves, white annual statice, pink strawflowers, white globe amaranth

1. Remove any husks, spray the corn lightly with gold paint, and allow it to dry.
2. Hot-glue a loop of gold cord to the top, to serve as a hanger.
3. Hot-glue the leaves and flowers to the top and bottom of the ornament in the order listed, using the photo as a guide.

Scotch Plaid Ornament

Materials
Acrylic spray, glue gun, thin red ribbon, seedheads from wild grasses, plaid ribbon, red and pink globe amaranth

1. Coat the cob with acrylic spray and allow it to dry.
2. Hot-glue a loop of thin red ribbon to the top.
3. Hot-glue the seedheads around the top.
4. Cut a piece of plaid ribbon long enough to circle around the top and hot-glue it to the corn.
5. Finally, hot-glue the globe amaranths in the center.

Scotch Pine

One of only three conifers native to Britain, the Scotch pine has 2- to 3-inch (5 to 8 cm) needles in bundles of two. It has been exported extensively to the United States for Christmas tree farms and reforestation.

⁂ Decoupage Eggs ⁂

Decoupage eggs are literally a cut-and-paste project, very simple to do. They are, of course, as fragile as eggshells.

Materials

White eggs, fork or straight pin, white glue, decorative paper, small paintbrush, clear acrylic spray, 9-inch (23 cm) piece of fine-gauge wire; small beads, spangles, or tassels; wire clippers or heavy shears

1. To empty out the egg, wash and dry it, then make a small hole in the narrow end, using a fork tine or a straight pin. Make a slightly larger hole in the wide end (now the bottom). Working over a bowl, blow on the top hole, forcing the white and yolk out of the bottom. Rinse the eggshell again and set it aside to dry.
2. Cut out small pieces of decorative papers—giftwrap, pictures from magazines, note cards, whatever is handy. Glue the pieces of paper to the egg.
3. When the glue is dry, coat the entire egg with clear acrylic spray. Apply a second and third coat of acrylic, allowing the eggs to dry after each application.
4. Insert the fine wire through the top and bottom holes in the egg. Add flat spangles, small beads, or a jingle bell at top and bottom.
5. At the top of the egg, twist the excess wire into a loop, twist the loop closed, and cut off the excess wire. Tie a piece of decorative cord or string to the wire loop to serve as a hanger.
6. At the bottom of the egg, wrap the wire end around the bottom bead or tassel and trim off the excess wire.

❊ PYRAMIDS ❊

These contemporary-looking, three-dimensional pyramids are easy to make.

Materials

Heavy mat board, razor knife, glue gun, acrylic paints, paintbrush, paint pens, glitter glue, craft gems, bead cap, bead, heavy thread, threads in various colors, colored tree icicles, needle

1. Using paper, pencil, and a ruler or straightedge, draw an isosceles triangle 4-1/2 inches (11 cm) on its long sides and 3 inches (7.5 cm) on its short side.

2. Trace the triangle three times onto heavy mat board and cut out the three triangles with a razor knife.

3. Using a clear glue stick, hot-glue the three triangles together along their long edges to create a pyramid, leaving the bottom open.

4. Paint the pyramid with acrylic paints, using whatever patterns of lines and squiggles appeal to you.

5. Lay a long bead of glitter glue along the edges where the three triangles meet. Add dots of glitter glue on the three surfaces. Add a sizeable "puddle" of glitter glue and place a craft gem in the center.

6. Glue the bead cap on top of the pyramid.

7. To make a tassel, form a 1-inch-thick (2.5 cm) bundle of 14-inch (35 cm) lengths of colored thread, plus a few colored Christmas tree icicles. Fold the bundle in half and wrap a piece of heavy thread around it about 1 inch from the fold. Knot the thread, leaving two very long tail ends.

8. Thread both long ends through the needle, so that you're working with a doubled thread, and bring the needle up through the top of the pyramid. Thread the bead onto the needle, push it down to the top of the pyramid, and knot the thread right above the bead, to hold it in place. Tie the ends of the thread in a loop to form a hanger.

�֍ MINI WREATHS ✖

Combine a few miniature wreath bases, a little glitter glue, some odds and ends, and a sense of fun, and you can whip up delightfully outrageous ornaments in no time.

Materials

4- or 5-inch (10 to 13 cm) vine wreath base, glue gun, glitter glue sticks, shiny cord, trinkets

1. Just wrap the wreaths with something long, thin, and shiny, hot-gluing the ends in place.
2. Hot-glue the trinkets of your choice to the wreath.
3. Examine the photo for examples to either embrace or avoid. Back row, left to right: 1) Gold tinsel mini garland plus red, gold, and silver plastic beads. 2) White buttons, white mini garland, and dollops of red glitter glue. 3) Plastic tube beads strung on floral wire and gold tinsel mini garland. 4) Multistrand telephone wire, gold mini garland, and gold jingle bells.

Front row, left to right: 1) Beads strung on floral wire and gold mini garland. 2) Purple metallic cord and lavender buttons. 3) Plastic beads, dollops of red glitter glue, and gold mini garland.

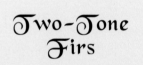

Two-Tone Firs

Many firs have needles with different colors on top and bottom. The Fraser fir is rich green above and blue below. The silver fir is dark green on top and silver underneath.

⁂ Marbled Ornaments ⁂

These memorable ornaments started out as inexpensive satin balls. They got their color from marbling, a craft that is becoming increasingly popular. To make them, you'll need the acrylic fabric paints available at any craft store, plus two items that are available only where marbling supplies are sold. One is aluminum sulfate, a white powder that acts as a mordant—that is, it makes paint bond with fabric. The other is methyl cellulose, a form of wood pulp, which is used to thicken water.

Materials

White satin balls, aluminum sulfate, clothesline and clothespins, methyl cellulose, household ammonia, 2 buckets or deep bowls, acrylic fabric paints, eye dropper, knitting needle or chopstick (or any object with a single long point)

1. Stir 1/2 cup (118 ml) aluminum sulfate into 1 gallon (4 l) of hot water until the powder is dissolved. Immerse each ball for 10 to 15 seconds, remove it from the mordant, and hang it to dry, using the clothespins to attach it to the clothesline.
2. Stir 4 tablespoons of methyl cellulose into 1 gallon of warm water. When the methyl cel has dissolved, stir in 2 tablespoons of ammonia. Pour this "bath" into a deep bowl or bucket and allow it to sit for about 12 hours. When you're ready to marble, pour clean water in the other bucket.
3. If there are loose threads on any of the balls, unwrap the stray end until you have a good "tail" of thread, tie it around the ball's hanger, and trim the end.
4. Pour each color of fabric paint into a small container and add clean water a little at a time until the paints are about the consistency of whole milk. Drop just a drop on the bath. If the paint sinks, add more water.
5. Skim the bath by drawing a strip of newspaper over it.
6. With the eye dropper, drop individual drops of paint onto the bath; they should float on the surface. Add drops of other colors until the surface is covered.
7. Holding the knitting needle vertically over the bath, insert the tip into the bath and move it back and forth, creating swirling patterns in the paint.
8. Holding a ball by its hanger ring, dip it straight down into the bath, immersing it completely. Then bring it straight up out of the bath.
9. Rinse the ball by dipping it in the bucket of clean water, then bringing it back out.
10. Hang the ball on the clothesline to dry. Skim the surface of the bath, add new drops of paint, and marble another ball. Continue in this fashion until you have as many as you want.
11. Check the hangers on the balls. If any are loose, pull them up to give yourself some working room and cement them to the balls with white craft glue.

✻ Glitter Glue Balls ✻

Go for baroque! To create insanely ornate ornaments, latch onto glitter glue sticks of many colors.

Materials
White satin Christmas balls, glue gun, glitter glue

1. Apply glitter glue directly to the Christmas balls, changing colors as you go along. Dots, vertical lines, wavy lines—live it up.

2. Work the top of the ball and let it cool, then work the bottom and let it cool, going back and forth until the ornament is overdone by any standard of sober good taste.

✻ Glitter Glue Snowflakes ✻

For this project you'll need one of the transparent glue pads available where glue guns and glue sticks are sold. The advantage of the pads is that hot glue won't stick to them.

Materials

Pencil, paper, glue pad, glue gun, glitter glue, decorative cord

1. Draw a basic snowflake design, using pencil and paper.
2. Place the drawing under the glue pad. Then draw your snowflakes in hot glue, following the lines of the original design.
3. Allow the snowflake to cool, then lift it off the pad.
4. Add a hanger of decorative cord.
5. If your tree is already full, you can press the snowflakes onto your windowpanes, where they will adhere nicely and serve as window decorations.

❋ Magnetic Ornaments ❋

Discount marts sell sheets of material that are magnetic on one side and sticky on the other—which means you can cut out the shapes of your choice, remove the protective sheet from the sticky side, and press on bits of decorative paper. After Christmas is over, pull off the hangers and stick the magnets on the refrigerator.

Materials

Sheets of magnetic material, bits of old Christmas cards, glittery paper, craft jewels, glue gun, glitter glue sticks, decorative cord

1. Cut the magnetic sheets into the shapes of your choice.
2. Peel off the protective paper from the sticky side of the magnet and press the bits of paper into it, creating a design as you go.
3. Decorate the ornaments with dots and lines of glitter glue; make some of the dots large enough to hold a craft jewel. Encircle the entire ornament with a bead of glitter glue.
4. Fold the decorative cord loosely in half and glitter-glue it to the back of the ornament.

❋ SPANGLE BALLS ❋

These brilliant ornaments will reflect every light on your tree.

Materials

Satin tree balls; shiny, round, flat spangles 3/4 inch (2 cm) in diameter; glue gun; clear and glitter glue sticks; narrow ribbon

1. Beginning at the bottom of the ball, hot-glue rows of spangles around it, using clear glue sticks and overlapping the spangles from side to side and from top to bottom.

2. When the ball is covered, encircle the metal ring at the top of the ball with five or six dots of glitter glue.

3. If desired, you can dot glitter glue on each spangle. The green ball in the center, for example, boasts dollops of red glitter glue on each green spangle.

4. Tie a piece of narrow ribbon to the ball's built-in loop to serve as a hanger.

❈ GOLD AND SILVER TREE ❈

Some of the best-looking trees rely on quantity as well as quality.
A riot of ornaments—with no branch left untouched—is delightful to look at…and look at…and look at. To achieve this effect,
combine the purchased ornaments you're especially fond of with
your own handcrafted decorations.

Patterned Gold Ball

Materials
Purchased glass ball, glitter, extra-
hold hairspray in pump bottle, bristle
or sponge brush with fine tip

1. Sketch several designs with
   pencil and scratch paper until
   you find one you like.
2. Pour some of the hairspray into
   a small bowl.
3. Dip the brush into the hairspray and paint a portion of the

design onto the ball.

4. While the sticky spray is still wet,
   sprinkle it heavily with glitter.
5. Continue in this fashion until the
   design is complete. While the balls
   shown have matching glitter, contrasting colors can be very effective.

Feather Ornament

Materials

Small white feather, lace ribbon

1. Tie the ribbon around the quill end of the feather.
2. Position the feather on a tree branch.

Miniature Package

Materials

Small box, patterned foil giftwrap, white craft glue, blue ribbon, white beads

1. Wrap the package with the giftwrap.
2. Glue the ribbon around the package in a cross shape.
3. Glue the white beads to the intersection of the ribbon.

Metallic Thread Ornament

Materials

Small piece of styrofoam in desired shape, metallic silver thread, white glue, narrow blue ribbon

1. Wrap the metallic thread around the foam base, securing the end under the first few wraps. As much as possible, wrap in the same direction, so that the threads are parallel on each section of the ornament.
2. When the foam is completely covered, secure the tail end of the thread with a tiny dab of glue on the center top of the ornament.
3. Tie the ornament with the blue ribbon, dividing it into four vertical segments. Finish with a bow, hiding any trace of the glue.
4. Add a loop of metallic thread, tying it underneath the blue ribbon.

❊ PAINTED GLASS ORNAMENTS ❊

Frosted glass ornaments are excellent for painting. On clear ornaments, the painted design shows through to the other side and distorts both sides. The balls above are decorated in designs reminiscent of the American Southwest.

Materials

Frosted glass balls, soft lead pencil, acrylic paints, narrow-tipped paint brush, narrow ribbon

1. Sketch your design on the ball in soft-lead pencil.
2. Paint the design in the colors of your choice.
3. Attach a hanger of narrow ribbon.

❋ SHELL TREE ❋

This elegant, gold-and-white tree displays a fine collection of seashells. Gold bows act as fillers.

Materials
Seashells, glue gun or drill with 1/16-inch (1.5 mm) bit, gold decorative cord, gold ribbon 1 inch (2.5 cm) wide, floral wire

1. Attach the shells to loops of decorative cord. If the shell has an opening, just thread the cord through the hole and tie it in a loop.
2. If not, you can drill one. The results are tidy, but you risk breaking some shells. The other option is to hot-glue the cord to the shell, using as little glue as possible and positioning it inconspicuously.

⁂ BEACH SANTAS ⁂

If you pick up small pieces of flotsam as you stroll along the beach, only to toss them in a drawer until you eventually throw them away, you now have something to do with them. Both shells and small pieces of driftwood make good Santas. Even grungy shells clean up well when they're bleached.

Clamshell Santas

Materials
Clamshells, household bleach, acrylic paints, paintbrushes, fine-tipped permanent markers, liquid "snow," glue gun

1. Wash the shells, scrape off any remaining debris, and soak them for two or three days in a mixture of one part bleach to three parts water. Allow to dry.
2. Paint Santa faces on the shells, giving them the personality of your choice. Use the permanent markers to draw the facial features. Add a textured band of "fur" on the cap, using one of the liquid-snow products that become three-dimensional when they dry.
3. Knot the ends of the ribbon to form a loop, and hot-glue it to the back of the shell.

Driftwood Santas

Materials
Driftwood, acrylic paints, paintbrush, fine-tipped permanent markers, clear acrylic spray

1. Rinse the sand and grit off the driftwood pieces and allow them to dry.
2. Paint the pieces to look like Santas, either as faces or as whole figures.
3. When the paint is dry, spray them with clear acrylic.

⁂ Shell Angels ⁂

The iridescent wings of these angels shimmer in the tree lights.

Materials

Shells, household bleach, power drill with 1/16-inch (1.5 mm) bit, acrylic paint or clear acrylic base with glitter, paintbrush, 5-inch (13 cm) length of brass wire, monofilament, white "pearl" bead 3/4 inch (2 cm) in diameter, matching bead cap, 4-inch (10 cm) length of iridescent paper ribbon, 3-inch (8 cm) length of pearl garland, tiny flat shell (optional), glue gun, tacky glue

1. Soak the shells in a solution of one part bleach to three parts water for two or three days. Allow to dry.
2. If you have a power drill, drill a hole through the end of the shell.
3. Paint the shell the color of your choice. If the shell is particularly attractive, don't paint it. Rather, brush on a clear acrylic base containing glitter. Allow to dry.
4. To make a halo, form a loop in one end of the brass wire.
5. For a hanger, shape the monofilament into a loop. Thread both ends of the monofilament and the straight end of the brass wire through the bead cap, then through the bead.
6. Insert the wire and monofilament into the hole in the shell. Working from underneath the shell, apply a large dollop of hot glue to hold the assembly in place.

   If you didn't drill a hole in the shell, hot-glue the head unit and the hanger to the back of the shell.
7. Untwist the paper ribbon and tie a piece of monofilament around the center, to shape it into wings. Hot-glue the wings to the back of the angel.
8. Place the center of the pearl garland in front of the angel's "neck." Wrap the ends around the neck and back to the front, to make the arms. Glue the arms to the front of the shell with tiny dabs of tacky glue. You may need to hold the garland in position until it dries a bit.
9. If desired, use tacky glue to attach a tiny shell between the angel's hands.

⁂ SEASHELL TABLE TREE ⁂

Finally: a way to use up all those shells you picked up at the beach three years ago. Besides, even the bathroom should have a Christmas tree.

Materials

Foam or paper cone 14 inches (35 cm) tall, low-melt glue gun, seashells, bath beads and hearts, narrow gold metallic ribbon, fine-gauge floral wire, narrow pink cord

1. Glue the shells onto the cone, covering it completely. Inset the bath beads and hearts as you go along.
2. To make a base, select a fairly flat shell large enough to hold the tree. Stabilize the large shell by hot-gluing small shells to the bottom of it where necessary to hold it level.
3. Glue the tree to the shell base.
4. Cut five lengths of the pink cord about 13 inches (33 cm) long and hot-glue their ends to the top of the tree. Allow the streamers to hang down the tree on all sides.
5. Make two bows from the gold metallic ribbon, wiring each one around the center to hold it together. Glue one bow on top of the tree and one at the base.

⚶ AGATE SLICES ⚶

If you've ever admired the rich colors and gorgeous patterns of agate, think Christmas; to become a tree ornament, an agate slice needs only a hanger. The inexpensive slices are available at stores that sell minerals, jewelry supplies, nature products, or even a wide range of gifts. Since agate is fairly heavy, select the smaller slices.

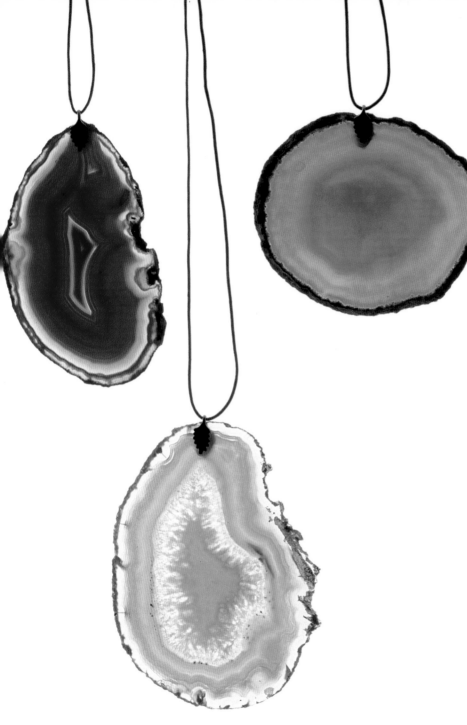

Materials

Agate slice, metal "feather" clasp, quick-setting epoxy, decorative cord

1. Wash and dry the agate, removing any glue left by price tags.
2. Bend a feather clasp into a U shape by bending it around a pencil, so that you get a smooth, round curve rather than an unpredictable kink.
3. Insert the edge of the agate slice into the hanger and use needle-nosed pliers to squeeze the clasp closed until both ends fit snugly against the agate. Remove the clasp from the agate.
4. Mix the two parts of the epoxy, following the manufacturer's instructions. Dab epoxy on both the agate and the clasp, where the two will meet, and insert the agate into the clasp. If there are any huge dollops of epoxy showing, try to wipe them off. Allow the epoxy to set.
5. Thread a loop of decorative cord though the hanger; gold-dyed leather cord is shown in the photo.

3. Continue in this fashion until the ball is covered with shavings.
4. To make a hanger, tie the cord in a loop and glue it to the ball.

Hanging Beads

Materials
Round, unfinished, wooden beads in 3 sizes, beads resembling children's blocks, acrylic paints in primary colors, paintbrush, heavy jute cord or yarn

1. Paint the beads with the acrylic paints, mixing the sizes and colors. Allow to dry.
2. String the beads on the jute cord. Knot the cord below the bottom bead and above the top bead, leaving a tail to tie to the tree.

Bead Garland

Materials
Oval, unfinished, wooden beads, black-and-white melon-shaped beads, red acrylic paint, paintbrush, jute cord or yarn

1. Paint the oval beads red and allow them to dry.
2. String the beads onto the jute cord, alternating the two types.
3. Knot the cord next to each end bead, leaving tails of cord on each end to tie to the tree.

A Is for Apple

Materials
Unfinished plywood letters, numbers, and apple, acrylic paints in primary colors, paintbrush, jute cord or yarn, glue gun

1. Paint the letters with the acrylic paints and allow them to dry.
2. Form pieces of the cord or yarn into loops and hot-glue them to the back of the ornaments.

✺ CRAYONS AND PAINT ✺

For a child's room, make a tree filled with childish things: bundles of crayons tied up with yarn, ornaments of crayon shavings, painted wooden beads and blocks, and the letters and numbers that the child is learning. You might add a juicy, red apple.

Crayon Balls

Materials
Old crayons, crayon sharpener, paper plate, brush, white glue, foam ball 2-1/2 inches (6 cm) in diameter, decorative cord

1. Sharpen the crayons until you have lots of shavings. Place the shavings on a paper plate.
2. Brush white glue onto a section of the ball and roll the glued section in the shavings. Press more shavings on the ball with your hand if you need to.

Recycling Christmas Trees

In the United States alone, almost 40 million Christmas trees are cut each year. If they all came from one tree farm, it would be the size of Rhode Island. The average tree is six to seven feet (1.8 to 2.1 m) tall and weighs 15 to 20 pounds (7 to 9 kg).

That's a lot of landfill.

Fortunately, tree-recycling efforts are springing up just about everywhere. The most common municipal solution is to grind the trees into wood chips, then use them as mulch and soil amendments for erosion control and water retention.

More exotic uses include sinking the trees into a body of water to provide reefs for young fish and as bulwarks against beach erosion: the trees trap sand and thus help build dunes. They can even help restore wetlands. Strategically placed, they break up wave action and slow the flow of water, allowing a wetland the peace and quiet it needs to support a colony of plant life.